CW00864688

ONLY TIME
COULD HEAL

ONLY TIME COULD HEAL

LISA HEBERLING-DEL VALLE

To order additional copies of this book, contact:
Xlibris
1-888-795-4274
www.Xlibris.com
Orders@Xlibris.com
814910

CHAPTER ONE

Incomplete

June 2, 2017

Lights, camera, action!

Male models were used to hearing those words, whether it was for photoshoots, fashion shows, or even talks shows. They were wanted everywhere; they could be welcomed anywhere.

That's how life was for Lucas Law: the famous twenty-five-year-old editorial model, who appeared in every fashion magazine known to man. He seemed to have such pure perfection looks: fluffy, wild light brown-highlighted hair that was an undercut shaved style, beautiful tanned skin, a five-foot-eleven figure with 7 percent body fat, and glowing hazel eyes.

Who knew a small-town guy from Fresno, California, could make it in Hollywood?

Knock, knock, knock.

Lucas looked into the mirror of his makeshift dressing room on the set of *DANICA: TALK NOW*, which was a low-key talk show, just a few miles away from the upcoming fashion show he was promoting.

He had to admit that he had it all, didn't he?

"You're on in four minutes!" A frantic voice came through the door.

Lucas took a deep breath and checked his phone, not seeing the point, since he never found the name he always hoped to find on the screen.

He put his phone on silent as he put it in his pocket of his faded black slacks and made sure his tight-fitting blue button-up dress shirt was not wrinkled before leaving the room.

The moment he opened the door, everything happened too fast. He was used to it. Everyone would grab him, get his makeup on, make sure he was hydrated, put gel on his teeth to make him smile, and that he had the booklet regarding the fashion show in hand.

Now he just waited for the cue.

One minute until the commercial break comes to an end.

He checked his cell phone absentmindedly, regretting it since it was clear, except for the time: 11:12.

"You're not supposed to have your phone on the set."

Lucas grinned as he turned to his longtime friend and fellow producer on the show they were doing. Alex is the one who was getting Lucas all the gigs before he was big enough to do it all on his own.

"Sorry, Mom. I'll remember for next time."

Alex rolled his blue eyes and leaned against the wall.

"Just make the show look good, dude."

"I know the drill."

Lucas put the phone back in his pants pocket.

"I don't know why you always have to check your phone," Alex continued. "You are obsessed with that phone . . ."

"You know why I do." Lucas sighed as the show was starting again, and now he just had to wait until Danica, the talk show host, called him on stage.

Alex rubbed his lips together.

"You need to move on, man."

"Her own parents haven't heard from her, Alex," Lucas whispered to his friend. "Something happened, and I need to know what."

"I know you do." Alex motioned to his chest. "That's why you still wear those rings."

Lucas subconsciously put his hand over his chest, where the chain that held a pair of wedding bands was.

"Let's welcome Lucas Law!"

Suddenly, an applause roared throughout the set.

Lucas straightened up and headed on stage, flashing his million-dollar smile to the live audience, and then he shook the hand of the host, Danica. She was a five-foot-four heavyset woman with a little too much bounce in her step, it was almost annoying. Lucas sat across her in a comfortable seat and gave another wave to the audience, who seemed to be screaming for his presence.

He had to admit that he never could get tired of that feeling.

"Lucas, Lucas, Lucas, nice to have you back on the show!" Danica told him, getting comfortable in her own chair. "Is it just me, or have you become sexier?"

The audience screamed once more as Lucas tried to blush. "Oh, Danica, it's definitely not you—I have definitely become much sexier," he joked as everyone laughed. "Honestly, though, I think it's just the tan."

"Me too!" Danica faked her smile. "So, Lucas, you didn't just come on my show to talk about your unbelievable charming smile?"

Lucas chuckled. "No, I did not." He pulled up the booklet that had him on the cover, shirtless, with the lettering in Broadway font: Jim Yang's Fashion Show. "I am going to be starring, along with other attractive models, in Jim Yang's new season runway show. It's going to be epic since it's also going to be live on TV."

"Oh my goodness, that's amazing!" Danica squealed as the audience cheered and clapped. "Third year in a row, you'll be the star of one of Jim Yang's summer show! That's a big honor. You've also been in his winter season's as well, correct?"

"Yes, yes, I have." Lucas gave her his whitened smile. "I can't get enough of Jim Yang's attire, and I don't think I ever will. Each season, he comes out with something that no one is wearing. He doesn't follow the status quo, he challenges the status quo. Any fashion designer like that will always have my dollar."

After another applause, Danica had a slight twinkle in her eyes.

"So tell us, Lucas, what's new in your life? Don't tell me 'same old, same old,' like you always do!"

Lucas shrugged. "I honestly don't have anything new to give out right now. I'm so focused on my career, and I have no time for any socializing."

Danica gave a little pout.

"Oh, sweetheart, I think it's time to do some matchmaking."

"It's not necessary, Danica," Lucas told her. "When I find that perfect girl, I'll know it's her."

"Well, it better happens soon, or we are going to play matchmaker!" Danica told him, teasing him.

… … … … … …

After the show was over, Lucas went back to the dressing room and shut the door behind him. He brought out the rings once more and gave the smaller one a peck with his lips.

He felt it. He was so close; he knew she was waiting for him to find her.

Bethany Johnson, his high school sweetheart to whom he proposed on graduation day; he helped her get to New York to follow her dream of being an actress, while he stayed behind in California to get his start in modeling. They had wedding plans made, and everything was set for him to move to New York with her, but he knew she was trying to find a better place for them to live.

Suddenly, after he sent her a text that the wedding bands were ready and he was going to pick them up, he never heard from her, except for a text that said, "This number is no longer in service."

The police tried to find her, but her apartment was already vacant.

Her bank accounts were cancelled.

She had disappeared.

Her own parents never heard from her.

Lucas never gave up hope. He went to New York in multiple towns for weeks at a time, but no luck. No one had ever seen or heard of Bethany Johnson in New York.

One theory was that she ran away because she failed at her acting career.

Another one was that she had an affair and ran away with her new lover.

The last one scared him the most: She had been taken by someone.

Some days he prayed for results that she was with someone else or that she was in hiding. If he was ever to find out she was being tormented every single day and night while he lived the cozy life, he could never live with himself.

Once more he checked his phone out of habit, but something wasn't normal.

An unknown number had called him.

Voicemail (1).

He immediately checked the message, bringing the phone to his ear, his heart racing.

"One new message: Lucas, this is Trey Unger, PI. I found your fiancée. Come to my office as soon as possible."

Lucas's eyes widened. He found her?

It was too good to be true!

Lucas had hired some private investigator weeks after Bethany went missing. If the police or her family and loved ones weren't going to help her, he sure as hell was. He was never going to give up!

And now he just had to hope she was alive. Just because Trey found her, that doesn't mean she's found alive.

"Please, God . . ." Lucas closed his eyes. "Let me bring her home."

… … … … … …

"Sit down, Mr. Law," the six-foot-four thin man with thick glasses and suspenders demanded as he sat down in his own chair across the desk.

He sure didn't seem like the private investigator type, but he was the best in the business. Trey waited until Lucas sat down across him before throwing him a manila folder.

"She changed her name."

Lucas couldn't open the folder fast enough as he saw her ID picture. She looked just the same, her hair was longer, but that's all.

There she was.

Her ID described her perfectly.

New York State
Driver's License
ID: 555 000 1232
Lou, Bethany
PO BOX 1313
Manhattan, NY 10033
Sex: F
HT: 5'2"
Eyes: BROWN
Hair: RED
DOB: 05/14/1992
Bethany Lou

Her picture was just so beautiful to him: her brown eyes shining, her strawberry blond hair flowing over her shoulders, her skin a perfect shade of light tan, and no trace of makeup on her skin.

Lucas swore he fell in love all over again.

"Look at the rest, Mr. Law," Trey said, looking interested.

Lucas was startled. He forgot that Trey was there. He kept his cool and turned the page. He saw her books. "Books? She's a writer?" He didn't even know she liked to write.

"Yes. She quit her theater career, that reason is unknown," Trey said, leaning back in his chair. "She became a writer soon after. She is famous for her books in New York."

"That's my girl." Lucas smiled lightly but then panicked. "She's not with someone or married, is she?"

As Trey leaned forward near him, Lucas held his breath, waiting for the heartache. "No."

Lucas let out a breath he forgot he was holding inside. "Oh."

"She's been single. No husband, no boyfriend, no kids, and no life." Trey frowned. "That's why it took me three years to find her. She has literally never left her loft in Manhattan . . . I'm only guessing that part because all they have there are lofts for the rich and famous. Since her PO box is in Manhattan, I'm only assuming that's where she lives."

Lucas saw a picture of her at a book signing, smiling at her fans. He ran a hand over her face, almost felt a tear escape his eye.

"What happened, my love?"

"Listen, she has a book signing tomorrow in a bookstore, where, apparently, fans are already lined up to see her," Trey told him. "I'm just saying if you want to talk to her, that would be a great place to go."

Lucas sharply looked up at him. "Give me the name of the store."

… … … … … …

"YOU'RE WHAT?"

Lucas winced at Alex's loud yelling over his cellphone as he sat in the back seat of his taxi, heading toward the airport.

"Alex, calm down."

"Lucas, we go live in three weeks! If you aren't ready, then we have no show! You can't go chase fairytales at a time like this!"

"I'll be back in a few days," Lucas told him, holding the picture of Bethany waving to her fans in his hand. "I found her, Alex . . . I can't let this moment slip away."

"Fine, but if you're not back soon, I can't protect you."

"I know, I know," Lucas told him. "I'll be back."

"I hope you find her, Lucas. I really do. And I hope she's all right."

"Thanks, man."

Soon the two hung up.

Lucas felt butterflies in his stomach, not from fear of flying, since he flew around the world, but he just couldn't believe in less than twenty-four hours, he was going to be seeing his fiancée again. He wanted to know what happened. Why did she go missing? What happened to her?

Did someone hurt her?

No matter how much he fought the thoughts, he immediately assumed the worst. Was she raped? Kidnapped? Is she being held against her will still? Maybe someone brainwashed her to forget her family and friends? Her fiancé? Whatever the case may be, he was going to hold her and never let her go.

He couldn't fathom losing her again.

Lucas grabbed the rings around his neck again and sighed, feeling a sense of peace whenever he held them in his fingertips. It made him feel closer to Bethany.

He may have lied to Alex.

If he and Bethany start off where they left off, he wasn't going back home. He was going to quit his life in Hollywood and stay with Bethany in New York.

There was no way he could be separated from her ever again. Three years without holding her in his arms, it was too much for him.

"I'm coming, sweet love," Lucas whispered as the taxi driver pulled up to the airport drop-off. "I'll be there soon."

As he waited for the drop-off/pick-up section of the airport to clear out so he could be let off, he sat alone with his memories of the girl he just wanted to spend his life with.

Sixteen years old, driver's license just attained that day, and no date to the winter formal; how lame could he be? He was a bit of a nerd: square glasses, long thin hair that he had in a ponytail, scrawny figure, and not-so-up-to-date clothes. He had been transferred to this high school in Temple City, California, this year, but has yet to achieve any friendships.

He went to his winter formal without a date. Maybe a chance to make a friend or two, he knew he wouldn't. He was the new guy and dressed geeky. Who would want to be friends with a guy like him in 2008?

He felt pathetic, standing close to the punch bowl and not a friend in the world.

Suddenly, she came up, the most beautiful girl he had ever laid his eyes on. She was very popular, and the guys always attempted to date her, but she was never interested. She was an amazing singer and actress, always getting the lead roles. She currently was going to star in Scarlett Letter as the main character. He thought she played it beautifully.

When she looked at him and smiled while getting her glass of punch, he felt his knees want to buckle, but he held himself together. Suddenly, she grabbed a second cup and poured a glass. She walked over to him with both cups, handing him one of them.

"Hi there," her velvet voice said as she took a quick sip of her punch after he took the cup.

She was dressed in a sparkly white dress that reached her ankles. Along with the small shimmering crown on her head from winning Winter Princess, her long strawberry blond hair with curls was flowing over her shoulders; her makeup done tastefully, not too overdone. Her light brown eyes gazed into his, melting his heart.

His heart raced. Did she know she was talking to him?

"Um . . . um, hi."

She giggled. "You looked pretty lonely over here. You're here alone?"

"Of course." He chuckled nervously. "New guy here, so I don't know anyone."

She grinned. "Well, you know me now. I'm Bethany Johnson, tenth grade."

He was still in quite a bit of shock as he shook her hand.

"I'm Lucas Law, tenth grade as well."

"Nice to meet you, Lucas." Bethany charmed as she blushed a little. "Now you have a new friend."

Lucas nodded. "I guess I do. Um . . ." He couldn't believe he was getting so bold. "I haven't made any friends since I started school here last week."

"I don't have many friends," Bethany told him. "I try to keep to myself."

"I'm surprised since you're so popular." Lucas mentally slapped himself. "I mean, um . . . you were voted Winter Princess, so I just figured you were so popular with friends or something . . ."

When will he shut up?

Bethany just laughed and shrugged. "I don't know. If I am, it's only because I try to be nice to everyone, but I really rather be alone."

"Do you want to be alone now?" he asked causally, but mentally, he was pleading with her to say no.

Bethany shook her head as she smiled sweetly at him. "You're an exception . . ."

He swore his stomach did some flips.

"Hey, this dance is nice but kind of lame, and I was about to take off, so um . . . do you want to go get some dinner?"

Bethany nodded. "Sure, I'd love to."

"I went for my license today, so I have my dad's convertible," *Lucas tried to say coolly.*

Bethany took his hand as they left the gymnasium and left the dance toward the car.

"Convertible or minivan, if you're in it, I can't wait."

That was the moment knew he wanted to be with her forever.

"Can I help you, Mr. Law?" the girl at the front desk of the airport asked as she was blushing madly as Lucas stepped up to her counter.

Lucas flashed her a fake smile. "One-way ticket to New York, please."

"Of course. What time?" she asked, typing in some information.

"As soon as possible," Lucas told her as she nodded.

"How does thirty minutes from now sound?" she said, not looking up at him because of nervousness.

"Perfect," Lucas said, looking at his watch.

"Seeing anyone special?" she asked, still blushing.

"My long-lost love."

CHAPTER TWO

Breakaway

June 3, 2017

After the seat belt light went off, all the passengers went about their business by taking off their seat belts, using the lavatories, getting their cell phones or other electronics out.

Our model on board was staring at pictures, the pictures he'd kept on his cell phone for many years. Lucas had a brand-new phone off the shelf, but the photos have been transferred from phone to phone.

Photos from the first date he and Bethany ever went on in 2008 in the tenth grade of high school.

Then their first anniversary in 2009.

Their senior prom in 2010.

Their one-month trip to Greece in the summer of 2011.

His family reunion in 2012 that they both attended.

Their first sips of alcohol on her twenty-first birthday in 2013.

College graduation day in May 2014, the day he proposed.

And then there was the last picture he ever took with her, the day he helped her move into her apartment in New York City, and then he was back on a plane to Hollywood, but he vowed once they married in September 2014, he would move there with her.

And that was the last time he ever saw her, kissed her, and told her in person how much he adored her.

He never wanted anything more than to hear her voice once more or to hold her in his arms so he could have proof that she was alive and safe.

Lucas had never told anyone how much his heart wrenched with agony every single night he had to go without knowing if Bethany was okay.

"You going to visit your girl?" a gruff voice said from next to him.

Lucas sighed, putting the phone face up on the table before him and looked out the window.

He saw the clouds cover the wing of the plane on his side, which almost felt relatable. He felt like he was clouded from the world.

"Yeah," he whispered, not being able to regain his normal tone of voice. "I haven't seen her in three years."

"Whoa, son," said the older man who looked to be in his sixties. He pointed to the picture. "She's a gorgeous one. How can you stay away from her that long?"

Lucas looked at the picture again as well, looking onto Bethany's smiling face. Something just seemed off though; she looked like she was hiding something, hiding her true feelings of sadness.

"She went missing," Lucas gulped. "I can't believe I've found her after all this time. I can't believe she's alive and safe."

"Oh my. Something must've happened for her to go missing like that," the man said. "Were you married?"

"Engaged. Together for seven years." Lucas finally peeked at the man who was staring at him with concern. "I've missed her more than anything in the world."

"I'm sure." The man took his hand out of his jacket pocket and reached for Lucas's hand. "I'm Rick Moore, I'm going to visit my daughter in New York."

Lucas shook his hand with a hard nod. "Nice to meet you. I'm Lucas Law."

"Oh, I know who you are, kid." Rick pointed across the aisle. "The magazine that young lady is reading has your name on the cover. Nice abs."

Lucas blinked. "I'm uncomfortable."

"Look, son, all I'm saying is I know who you are." Rick grinned at him. "If I was hitting on ya, you would know."

"Lovely," Lucas grumbled.

"Are you nervous?" Rick asked him, getting back on topic.

Lucas nodded. "Very. I haven't seen her in three years. I don't even know what happened. I've never been with anyone else though. I almost still consider us engaged." He took the wedding bands out of his shirt. "I still have the bands that I picked up three years ago. Every time I hold them, I feel closer to her."

"Were you ever worried she wasn't alive?" Rick asked.

"Every day." Lucas sighed. "I knew she was alive because I love her so much, I almost felt her heartbeat, but the thought of not knowing if she was safe, it was unbearable. I don't even know how I've lived three years not knowing."

"Are you scared of the reason?"

"Yes. I'm scared she was raped or something." Lucas put his hand on his face, trying to not relay images of his tiny fiancée being forced upon. "There are so many nightmares that have kept me up at night. I can't deal with not knowing anymore. I just need to see her face. Even if she doesn't feel the same anymore, I don't care. As long as she's alive and safe, that's all I care about. Yes, I would love to start things where we left off, but even if we can't, I just want to hear her voice."

"How'd you find her?" Rick asked, out of curiosity.

Lucas chuckled. "Believe it or not, I hired a private investigator."

"Smart." Rick leaned back in their first-class seats. "My wife died last year, and I am kind of like you. I just want to hear her voice one more time."

"I'm sorry for your loss," Lucas said sympathetically. "You know, Rick, this is the first real conversation I've had with someone about my feelings since Bethany went missing."

Rick nodded. "I'm sure, being a famous celebrity, you don't get much time to socialize."

"It's not even that though," Lucas told him. "I just felt like if I told anyone my situation, it would all become real."

"The fact is that it was real," Rick told him. "Cherish this girl. You have a second chance now. Don't waste it."

"You're right, I won't." Lucas smiled. "Thanks, man."

Soon he heard the snores of Rick, and he thought that would be a good idea to catch some sleep before they landed in two more hours.

Lucas sighed deeply, getting comfortable in his large leather seat. He put his earphones on, turned on his music, and fell into a deep sleep.

As he finished cutting down the last of the boxes from the move for his fiancée, Lucas stretched his arms around and arched his back in attempt to pop it. He looked around, and the place looked so small and lonely. It was a small apartment, not even a bedroom. It was just a little place to stay for someone who was just getting their start. It wasn't in the best of neighborhoods in New York City, but it's where Bethany chose to live so she can save up to live somewhere better.

He was so afraid something would happen to her while he was going back to Hollywood, but he knew once Bethany had her mind set on something, she wasn't going to be swayed.

The picture on the nightstand by her air mattress bed was a portrait of him and her on their graduation day as he was down on one knee. She was in tears. That was the day she said "yes" to his proposal. Lucas had no regrets. He never thought of anything being more perfect than spending the rest of his life with Bethany.

Yes, they were young, but he had no doubt in his mind about spending his life with her.

She was so perfect.

Sweet.

Amazing.

And so very patient.

He just hoped he could survive until the new year when they would wed, and he would move to New York.

How was he going to survive so far away from her?

Bethany suddenly appeared from the bathroom, dressed and ready.

It was easy to tell she had been crying, but it was worse because Lucas knew she was sick. Lately, she had been getting lightheaded and nauseous.

It worried him so.

Yes, Bethany did get sick quite a bit because of her chronic illness of lupus she suffered from since she was nineteen, but this was different.

Bethany tried to reassure him she would see a doctor if it didn't go away.

Lucas wished he could stay and be there for her.

Bethany looked so upset about being separated.

"Do you have to go?"

Well, that broke his heart.

Lucas sighed deeply and walked up to his petite fiancée, wrapping his arms around her in a loving embrace.

"I told you say the word, and I'll stay."

Bethany shook her head. "No, no, I'm sorry. I'm just being a baby."

"Bethany, you're not a baby," Lucas said firmly, putting her lose hairs behind her ear. "You're such an amazing person for taking on this big adventure. I can't help but admire you. I wish I could take this big of a risk."

"I'm scared," Bethany whimpered. "I've never been on my own before."

"I know." Lucas kissed her head. "We're getting married in seven months. I promise I'll be moving here soon enough. I'll have everything ready to go right after we say 'I do,' and then we'll live happily ever after here in New York."

"I promise I'll find somewhere else to live," Bethany told him, cringing at the tiny apartment.

"Just promise me you'll be safe," Lucas told her, sitting down carefully on her air mattress, and then pulled her onto his lap. "I don't ever want to hear you were hurt in any way."

"You won't." She pecked his cheek. "I'll be all right."

They sat in silence in that position, staring into each other's eyes.

They were dreading that only in a couple hours they would be separated for seven months.

Little did they know it would be three years before they would see each other again.

"I love you, Bethany," Lucas whispered.

"I love you too."

Suddenly, their lips connected, and Lucas pulled Bethany onto the mattress with him, slipping her underneath him as they continued to kiss of passion.

Lucas let a tear slip from his eyes as he peacefully woke up from his slumber. He swore he could feel Bethany's presence with him during those type of dreams.

That dream wasn't made up though. It was his memory of the last time of intimacy he shared with Bethany.

It was the last time they had become one.

"Attention, passengers, we will be landing in New York City in twenty minutes. Let's head back to our seats and buckle our seat belts so we can land."

Lucas buckled his seat belt and put his tray into its upright position.

He looked at Bethany's face one last time before he turned off his phone.

… … … … … …

When Lucas booked his tickets, he didn't take into consideration the traffic New York had.

He was miles away from the bookstore, but it was rush hour; bumper-to-bumper traffic.

The taxi he was in was currently at a complete stop.

Lucas saw the time: 12:49 p.m. Bethany's book signing ends at one!

If he doesn't make it on time to see her, he'll lose her again!

He could not handle this!

"How far are we?" Lucas asked, almost in panic as the clock turned to 12:50. "The place I'm going has a book signing, and it ends at one!"

"Then why didn't ya take a cab to your destination earlier?" the driver yelled from the front seat. "Ya kids think ya can leave ten minutes before and still make it on time? So impatient!"

Lucas sat back in his seat, whimpering. His heart was racing.

The driver saw his frantic state and rolled his eyes. "We are two miles away."

Lucas closed his eyes, trying to hold his emotions in place.

There was no way they would make it. Even if he ran, he still won't make it. The traffic hadn't moved in ten minutes.

Suddenly, he opened his eyes after hearing a loud nose. It sounded like a tunnel! He saw the subway entrance was right next to him.

Crosby stop was the next stop!

All he had to do was get on the subway and stop right at Crosby exit, and then he'd be right there to the bookstore.

Lucas took out a few twenties out of his wallet and then jumped out of the car, sliding his small duffel bag onto his shoulder.

He raced to the subway stairway and jumped each step in glee, praying he would get there on time.

He received his ticket and practically jumped over the gate. He made it to the right stop, barely making it on board.

He grabbed onto one of the poles. It was crowded within the subway car, but he paid no heed.

He just couldn't believe he was so close to the woman he lost three years ago.

He was going to hold her.

If he could get there on time!

It was 12:56 now!

"In a hurry?" a young blond girl said, smirking at him. "I can slow you down."

"No, you can't," Lucas said, exasperated. "I'm on a mission."

Finally, the doors opened after they came to a stop, and he was the first one out, pushing through everyone to get up the stairs to the street above.

Everyone was yelling at him to slow down, but nothing could get him to slow down.

Soon he had the bookstore in his sights. His heart raced from anxiety and adrenaline.

This was it!

"Bethany?" Lucas called out with hope as he ran into the building. He saw the sign that had Bethany's new book on it getting taken down by an employee as another employee was cleaning the table. "No . . ." He was too late.

He looked around and saw no sign of her.

His heart broke as he realized this was all for nothing. He missed his chance. He was too slow.

"I love how Bethany Lou rides in a limo!" Lucas heard a high-pitched voice said from next to him.

Two teenage girls were looking out the glass window in awe.

"She's so classy!"

"Seriously! I love her!" the other girl said.

Lucas quickly looked out the window as well and saw someone opening the backdoor for a strawberry blond woman. The woman was getting into the back as the man shut the door behind her.

Lucas felt a sharp pain in his chest. It was her!

"BETHANY!" he suddenly shouted, startling everyone around him.

He didn't waste time to apologize as he ran back outside.

He watched as the limo took off into traffic.

He can't let them get away!

If he lost the limo now, he'll never find her!

He didn't realize what he was doing until he did it. He raced in front of the limo before they could hit the traffic.

All Lucas remembered was the most painful feeling of metal being slammed into his body before he was sent flying onto the sidewalk once more. Oh, the pain.

"I'm an idiot," he groaned as he felt his whole body swore from the impact.

He heard a door slam as he looked to see the driver of the limo get out and rush to his side.

"Oh my god, sir, are you all right? Oh my god, you're Lucas Law! I'm so fired!"

Lucas couldn't speak as he groaned in pain. Everything just seemed to get blurry.

After hearing a crowd form, he closed his eyes, wishing this all to be a dream, just wishing he could be comforted by that one woman he had traveled almost three thousand miles to see once again.

"Oh my . . . Lucas?"

Lucas snapped his eyes wide open. His vision was blurry at first, seeing many dark figures before him, but soon his eyes adjusted as he felt two petite hands on either side of his face.

He saw her.

She was beautiful.

An angel.

Lucas smiled lightly. "Bethany."

Bethany was in complete shock of the situation. Her strawberry blond hair draped over her shoulders as her brown eyes stared into his hazel eyes.

He swore her lightly tanned skin glowed as the sun glared down at them. She was dressed in a short dress that was off the shoulder.

"Lucas, are you all right? How did you find me?" she asked in concern and amazement.

"You've been missing for three years, and you're worried about me?" Lucas grinned. "Get your priorities straight."

Bethany couldn't help but smile at him in a loving manner, taking his hand into hers.

Everyone around them were confused.

"I've been searching for you for so long," Lucas said, staying still on the sidewalk as they heard sirens near. "I couldn't let the limo drive away. I couldn't lose you again."

Bethany was touched.

Soon the ambulance was there, and they helped Lucas onto the gurney. "She's going with me." Lucas motioned to Bethany. "Please, please."

Bethany was still almost speechless but nodded. "Yes, I'll go with him."

"Are you sure, Ms. Lou?" her driver asked. "Do you know who this is?"

"I do," Bethany told him. "This is my fiancé."

Lucas couldn't believe his ears when he heard that. His heart fluttered with love and peace, a feeling he had been missing for too long. It was only then did he realize she still had her engagement ring on her left hand.

She never left him in the first place.

She was there all along.

As they put him in the back, Bethany was helped onto the bench in the back, and Lucas insisted on holding her hand the entire trip to the emergency room.

He was smiling through everything, ignoring his agonizing pain from being hit by a car.

Bethany stayed quiet, tears streaming down her cheeks. Even though the tears, she was still the most beautiful human being in the world to Lucas.

He missed this feeling of love.

Now that he had it, he never wanted it away ever again.

… … … … … …

"Breaking news! We all expect famous model Lucas Law to be preparing for his fashion show he is starring in for Jim Yang, right? WRONG! He actually was in New York City today! We don't know the whole story, but all we do know is that he jumped in front of a limo that contained famous author Bethany Lou! He is in stable condition at the hospital and in good spirits, sources say. We have word from the limo driver himself that Law was so demanding that Lou was to stay with him. When the driver asked why, Lou answered with that Law was her fiancé! We are all so confused yet so interested! We will keep you posted on the latest updates on our new favorite, dangerous couple: Luthany!"

Suddenly, the TV screen went dark as Bethany turned it off with the remote, and then she turned to Lucas with an amused look.

"Luthany?"

Lucas shrugged lightly, not trying to hurt himself.

"Can't choose everything."

Bethany rolled her eyes and stared at her fiancé.

"How did you find me?"

"Hired a private investigator a month after you went missing," Lucas told her with no hesitation. "I'm surprised your parents didn't do it before I did. Everything was just so weird. No one was freaking out. It was like they almost expected it." Lucas gave her hand a squeeze. "Baby, please, tell me what happened. I won't be angry, I promise."

Bethany shook her head. "No, not here, not now. I promise when you are released, I'll tell you before you go home."

Lucas looked at her like she had two heads.

"I'm not going home."

Bethany raised an eyebrow.

"What?"

"You have to be kidding!" Lucas was getting agitated. "I've been without you for three years! Three of the longest damn years of my life!"

"And?" Bethany shrugged. "I'm sure you've moved on by now, Lucas. No one waits for someone to come back that long."

"I do, okay?" Lucas was almost offended. "And I did."

Bethany looked at him with disbelief. "Lucas, you're a famous male model. Every time I passed the magazine stands on the street, you were always front cover, shirtless." She pointed out in an obvious tone. "You can't tell me that you've seriously never been with someone else."

Lucas was heartbroken. "How dare you . . . how dare you even think for a second that I would cheat on you?"

"You wouldn't have been cheating," Bethany said. "I ran away. I left you."

"We never called anything off, and even if we had, I would've fought through hell and back to keep you," Lucas told her in a harsh tone, wishing he could get out of bed.

"I don't believe you," Bethany told him.

"What?" Lucas was annoyed. He did not travel across the country for this!

"Lucas, you've been free for so long. How did you not?" Bethany asked him. "I wouldn't blame you, okay? I won't get upset. I won't get jealous. I've expected it. Of course, I didn't think I'd ever see you again, but that's beside the point."

Lucas shook his head. "You're unbelievable."

"How so?" Bethany looked at him in disbelief. "I'm telling you that it's okay."

"I'm telling you that I never gave up on you," Lucas growled at her.

"There's no way, Lucas." Bethany frowned. "No man can be alone for almost three years and be single or at least not get some action."

"Action?" Lucas shouted. "Action of what? I would not ever have sex with another woman! I'm engaged to you! I'm loyal to you!"

"Lucas, I don't believe you," Bethany said.

"You don't, huh?" Lucas shrugged. "Fine. Here's your proof."

Suddenly, he reached for the chain he hadn't taken off since the day he lost contact with her and took the rings into his hand, grabbed her hand harshly, shoved her ring on her finger next to her engagement ring.

He let her go and put his on his ring finger.

He saw her face shocked.

"I kept those around my neck since the day I picked them up from the jeweler. Whenever I felt anxious or alone, or absolutely terrified of what could've been happening to you at that very moment because I didn't know if you were safe or not, I held these things in my fingertips, praying that you were all right. They always gave me comfort and made me feel closer to you."

Bethany was out of words.

Suddenly, the doctor and nurses came in to check on Lucas, so Bethany backed up to the window seat. She took the wedding band off and examined it.

She couldn't believe her eyes, it was the wedding band she had picked out all those years ago.

She noticed it was engraved on the inside.

She squinted to read the small cursive print.

Forever & Always

Bethany couldn't contain her emotions after that, but when the doctor walked up to her, she wiped away her tears and put the wedding band back on her finger.

"I'm sure this is hard for you, Ms. Lou," the doctor said. "Almost losing your significant other is scary. Now I know you two are currently living on opposite sides of the country, but Mr. Law here cannot fly for another week."

Bethany figured what he was saying and nodded.

"Yes, sir. I'll keep him safe."

"Thatta girl." The doctor patted her shoulder before the nurses began to take the monitors off the injured man.

Lucas buttoned up his dress shirt, staring at his long-lost fiancée as she stared out the window, fiddling with her engagement ring and now her wedding band next to it.

Tears were silently going down her face as she tried to hold everything inside.

Lucas's heart broke all over again for her. She was hiding something from him, and it was tearing her apart.

He couldn't just let her stand there and suffer.

He walked up to her slowly and wrapped his arms around her from behind, and she let herself breakdown.

Bethany sobbed violently as he held her.

"How? I don't understand how you didn't give up on me."

Lucas comforted her the best he could.

"I love you. I've loved you since I was sixteen years old. How could I ever give you up?"

27

"I'm a monster!" Bethany shrieked. "I've done you so wrong!"

"How have you done me wrong?" Lucas asked softly. "Bethany, I don't know what happened to you. I don't. I want to know, but I know you'll tell me when you're ready."

Bethany sniffled through her tears. "It's horrifying."

Lucas felt like shaking it out of her, but he held his emotions in and took a deep breath.

"Beth, listen, you didn't do me wrong. Something traumatizing happened to you, I don't know what, but it's something serious, something that scared you to the point you felt you needed to walk away."

Bethany looked up at him.

"It's not that I didn't trust you. I just didn't want to tell you because it'll break your heart."

Lucas wrapped his arms around her once more and sighed into her hair.

"Take your time."

Then he kissed her cheek, something Bethany hadn't felt in so long. It made her heart flutter with joy.

Soon they separated, and Bethany sighed. "Well . . . we better get going."

"Is your house close?" Lucas asked her.

"Depends on your definition of close." Bethany giggled as she wiped her tears away.

Lucas nodded. "I'm kind of scared to know what that means."

Bethany laughed as they went to leave.

"You'll find out right now."

CHAPTER THREE

Behold

June 3, 2017

Horns were honking down the bumper-to-bumper Manhattan traffic.

Lucas began to understand why Bethany said he'll find out how far away she lived from the hospital!

They had been in the taxi for an hour, but it usually could only take twenty-five minutes to get from New York City to Manhattan.

Bethany didn't live too far from the hospital, but in New York, it could mean the difference between a few miles away to a few hours away.

If he wasn't still sore from being hit by the limo, Lucas would've suggested they walked or took the subway.

From his seat next to Bethany, he could tell she was emotionally fragile and couldn't comprehend the busy day she's had.

Her face was cleaned up from all her crying earlier, but her heart was still broken.

Lucas has begged her to tell him what happened to her, but she said to give her a little bit of time to figure out how to explain everything to him.

It was a start.

Finally, they pulled up to a large building that had a doorman outside, waiting for anyone who was given access to go up into the very wealthy building behind him.

Bethany rushed to the other side of the taxi, helping Lucas stand up from the vehicle, and then swung his duffel bag over her shoulder.

He grabbed his cheap cane that he would have to use for the next couple of days as he tried to gain his strength back and followed Bethany to the doorman, who smiled at her.

"Hi, Jeffrey," Bethany greeted him, faking a smile. "This is my . . . well . . . my fiancé, Lucas."

Jeffrey raised his eyebrows as he shook Lucas's hand. "Fiancé? My, oh my, what kind of day have you had, Ms. Bethany?"

Bethany giggled as Lucas blushed. "It's a long story."

"I'm sure I'll read it in your next novel." Jeffrey smiled.

Soon the two left Jeffrey at the front door as they walked in and headed straight for the elevator.

Next to the elevator was the mail slots, which appeared to only have twenty.

"Why are there so few mailboxes?" Lucas asked in curiosity after Bethany reached into the slot that said "16" to get her mail.

"There are only twenty floors," Bethany answered, leading him to the elevator as she lifted the gate up with ease. "Each one of us has our own floor."

"Really?" Lucas nodded as they stepped onto the elevator, and Bethany put the door back down safely and then pressed "16." "So I'm guessing you live on floor 16?"

"Loft 16, yes," Bethany told him as they began to go up. "It's just enough room for me and Loki."

Lucas was officially confused. "Loki?"

Instead of answering him, Bethany opened up the elevator doors and let him step inside before she closed it.

As soon as Lucas looked around, he saw something move on the couch.

His eyes widened as he saw a giant black dog step down with ease from the cushioned couch and stare at him.

Lucas gasped, "What the hell is that?"

Bethany giggled as she came up next to her fiancé. "This is Loki, my two-year-old Great Dane."

Loki gave out a grunt.

Lucas faked a smile. "Greetings." He looked over to Bethany. "I think Goliath came back as your dog."

31

Bethany rolled her eyes. "He's only 120 pounds." She cooed at Loki, who slowly walked up to her. "He's just a baby."

Lucas's jaw dropped.

"That baby is taller than you if it stood up on its back legs."

Bethany ignored him as she played with Loki's ears.

… … … … … …

Lucas sat out on the balcony, just taking in the sights of Manhattan, New York.

He had heating pad on his back, ice pack on his head, while everything else seemed to still be numb.

He was resting comfortably in Bethany's patio furniture couch, thankfully that reclined so his sore legs could be elevated.

He heard the chilly wind hitting the wind chimes, but he loved it. He loved the cold.

He remembered it was hard for Bethany to be anywhere cold because of the low blood pressure she had been dealing with since they met in high school.

Soon Bethany stepped out into the balcony and then cooed at the sight.

Lucas rolled his eyes as he looked to his side, where Loki was resting on his lap and stretched out onto the couch, taking over almost the whole piece of furniture.

He found out Loki was rescued by Bethany off the streets as a pup. What a pup, huh? More like a 120-pound monster to him.

And he had to say this was the laziest dog he had ever met in his life!

Bethany had a tray with iced tea in her hands as she placed it gently onto the glass table that was beside him so he could have easy access to it.

Lucas smirked. "Quite fancy."

Bethany blushed. "Sorry. I haven't had another human being in my loft before, so I'm a little uneasy."

"I understand." Whew. That meant she hasn't been with another man.

"You should call your parents," Bethany suddenly stated. "I'm sure they've seen the news."

Lucas sighed. "I will, I will, but, Beth, I really want to know what happened."

Bethany rubbed her lips together and nodded. "Can I tell you after you call? It's going to be a long, long explanation, and there's more to add as well."

It terrified him already to think of other things his fiancée had gone through while he was living his dream in Hollywood.

How could this have happened?

They had such a perfect relationship. Now it was torn apart by some traumatic experience Bethany had years ago.

He watched her go back into the house to give him some privacy. He realized what a fool he was back then.

How could he have possibly let his 112-pound, five-foot-two fiancée live in New York alone?

How?

What kind of man was he? Not one at all, according to the current circumstances.

She was a small woman, very petite. She was tough, though, but not bulletproof.

How could he have failed her like this?

He decided to take out his phone, seeing so many missed calls.

The calls were mostly from his manager, Alex, and one from his parents; actually, it was a text message from his parents.

Text message from Dad: *Hey son! Heard your drama going on in New York! Can't stay out of the spotlight, can ya? Please call us soon to explain! Thanks!*

Lucas chuckled.

His parents were the best. They never freaked out about anything.

He decided to video chat them, so he pressed "Video Call" and waited, checking if he had anything in his teeth while he waited for his dad to answer.

Suddenly, his father popped onto the screen, and he chuckled. "Your teeth are pearly perfect, son."

Lucas looked a bit embarrassed. "Thanks. Hey, so I'm in New York, by the way."

His dad rubbed his hand on his bald head and rolled his eyes. "Are you now? I didn't realize since you and Bethany are all over the news! How is she? I see she changed her last name, but I recognize her anywhere."

"She's doing very well, Dad." Lucas shrugged. "I think she's lonely over here by herself."

"Did she tell you what happened?"

"Nope." Lucas sighed. "She said she'll explain everything when I get off the phone with you guys. She wanted me to call you first to let you know I was all right."

His father grinned. "I always loved that girl. Anyways, son, when she tells you, please do not get angry, do you hear me? What happened to her was out of her control."

Lucas paused and had wide eyes. "Why are you talking like you know?"

"Because we both know about what happened!" Suddenly, his mother with her permed hair came into view and straightened her glasses to see her son. "Listen, she told her parents, who told us, and after Bethany went missing, the four of us made a pact that Bethany would tell you on her own time."

"You guys knew this whole time, and you didn't tell me?" Lucas yelled. "How could you? You knew how much I missed her! I could've helped her! So that explains why Bethany's parents never went searching for her."

"Yes, they knew she disappeared to do some healing. They didn't know she would take this long, but something so traumatic can make a woman so depressed and vulnerable," his mom explained. "Please be very patient with her. She's strong and tough, but even the sturdiest of women can fall sometimes. That's why we love so much. We need our men to pick us back up again."

Lucas thought about everything that just occurred and nodded. "Okay. I understand. Thanks, Mom. Thanks, Dad."

"In a few days, please give us a call back so we can talk to Bethany," Lucas's dad said with a smile.

His mom nodded in agreement. "Yes, please! I've missed her so much. Nothing has been the same since she disappeared."

"I will." Lucas then smirked. "I'm doing fine from being hit by a car, thanks for asking."

Both of his parents rolled their eyes.

"Please, don't bring that up," his father said.

"I had to tell my friends in the book club you were a stunt man because it was so stupid!" his mother said into the camera.

Lucas raised an eyebrow. "Hey, some might call that an action of romance."

Suddenly, his parents burst into uncontrollable laughter.

Soon they hung up after exchanging goodbyes, and he heard Bethany's sliding glass door open and shut.

She saw him off the phone and walked over. "I ordered some Chinese food." She looked at her watch. "It should be here in about an hour."

"Fantastic." Lucas didn't realize how hungry he was until his stomach suddenly growled.

Bethany gulped. "Is this a good time to talk? I think I've gathered up enough courage."

"Anytime and all the time is a perfect time to talk." Lucas smiled, but inside, he was severely nervous.

She made Loki get off the couch and go to his large bed by the couch, and she took a seat close to Lucas. He took her hand once she was comfortable and gave it a squeeze.

"Take your time, okay?"

Bethany nodded. "I might cry."

"That's fine," Lucas whispered.

Bethany took a few big breaths before continuing, "Um . . . I'll try to start from the beginning. After you left when I moved here, I found out I was three months pregnant with our child."

Suddenly, the world stopped spinning for Lucas.

The scenarios that ran through his head were indescribable.

She was pregnant. Where's the child?

How could she not have told him?

WHAT HAPPENED?

"I wanted to tell you, but I knew you so well. You would've stopped your rising career of modeling for me and the baby. I didn't want you to give it up just yet." Bethany sighed. "So I kept it a secret for five more months."

Lucas had no words to say as he listened intently. He never let go of her hand.

"On Thanksgiving Day, I was going down to a friend's house for a get-together with the cast of the show I was in because they wanted to host a Thanksgiving meal. I was only outside the building when someone tried to rob me. I didn't have my purse or anything because I only carried the cash I needed to get there, which was only a few bucks." Suddenly, the trembling became noticeable, so Lucas scooted closer to her as he fought through his sore muscles and his racing heart. "I told the guy I didn't have any money left, but he dragged me into the alley and wouldn't stop punching me and kicking me. I was on the wet ground, my face in a dirty puddle, and he wouldn't stop."

Now the tears start for both of them.

Lucas whimpered, "No . . ."

"When he was done, my friends came looking for me after, and I was crawling out of the alleyway by then, bleeding. I was bleeding to the point I was halfway dead." Bethany sobbed. "I couldn't save the baby at all! She was stillborn! She didn't stand a chance from the beating he put on her! I gave birth all alone in the hospital to a stillborn child! All because that man wanted a few bucks, which I didn't have! He killed my daughter for a couple of dollars!"

Lucas stayed quiet in his own tears as he leaned his head on her shoulder, rubbing the back of her neck in some feeble attempt to give her support, although he felt like nothing he could do at this point could make her feel better.

"If I could see him now, I would ask him, 'Was it worth it?'" Bethany sniffled away her tears, but only more came. "I was so damaged and alone, and I couldn't tell you afterward because I knew you would've hated me for not telling you in the first place! I was going to tell you when I went home for Christmas, but . . . but I screwed up. I lied to you."

Suddenly, Lucas couldn't hold himself back as he wrapped his arms around her waist, pulling her into his lap, and cradled her fragile body in his arms. "I love you so much." He didn't know what else to say. He had absolutely no words to tell her except that. "I love you. I love you more than anything in the world. I'm so glad you're okay. I'm so glad he didn't take you away."

Realizing he didn't hate her, and he was more worried about her life than anything, Bethany let herself break down into sobs once more in his hold like she did earlier that day.

"I just wanted to be a mom! I know we were so young, but we would've loved her so much! I was so ready for her! I wanted to be her mom so bad!"

Lucas continued to rock her back and forth, not seeing any calmness in sight.

··· ··· ··· ··· ···

After a while, the food came, and they ate, but Bethany suddenly was eating very little. He figured it was from the stress of telling him what happened.

He wished she didn't have to go through all of it all alone. He was upset that his parents didn't tell him what happened.

How could this have happened?

And why couldn't he have been there for her?

Everything seemed to be falling apart around him.

He just wished he knew *who* did the attack on his fiancée; the vengeance he felt he needed to fulfill was undeniable.

He couldn't imagine how much coldness a man had to have to attempt to kill an eight-months pregnant woman. A heartless, selfish, demented man, that's who.

"Lucas?"

Lucas snapped out of his thoughts as he tried to sit up to look back at Bethany, who was in the kitchen, but he couldn't.

She immediately came to his side, sticking a pillow behind his back to give him more comfort.

"Thanks, my love," he whispered in pain.

She nodded. "Lucas, I have a doctor's appointment tomorrow. Do you think you'll be okay here without me?"

His eyes shot to hers. "Doctor's?"

"Yes." She sighed. "I've been having some health problems."

Now the sharp pain in his chest came back.

When will all these awful things stop tormenting his fiancée?

"They're just trying to get me back to normal, but my lupus is getting pretty rough." She shrugged, as if it was not a huge deal to him. "Lucas, I know earlier you said you didn't plan on

38

going home, but seriously, though, what are you going to do? You have that show coming up."

"I don't care," Lucas told her firmly.

"Look, Lucas, we need to talk about this." Bethany sat next to him on the couch. "Yes, we are still engaged, but shouldn't we be talking about if we still need to be or—"

"What do you mean?" Lucas asked with worry. "You don't want to be engaged or be with me?"

"Well, I don't know." Bethany looked tired. "I just don't want you to feel that now that you found me, you have to stop everything to be with me."

"I have searched for you for almost three years!" Lucas shouted.

"I know, but—"

Lucas put his hand on her mouth gently and made her stop. "Let me finish. I don't think you realize how much I searched for you." He took his hand off her lips and put his hands on either side of her face. He leaned closer to her, forgetting the agonizing pain his body was in. "I never changed my phone number, e-mail address, or anything because I wanted you to be able to find me if you ever could or wanted to. I came to New York City in January 2015 to search and passed out flyers of you on it with my phone number."

"You did?" she whispered.

"Yes." He rubbed her cheek softly with his thumbs, not taking his eyes off her eyes. "I left two weeks later because of work, but I left thousands of flyers everywhere. I came back a second time to search, but all my flyers were gone by March 2015." He gulped, attempting to hold back his emotions. "Then in July 2015, I came here to Manhattan. I passed by this building hundreds of times in those two weeks I was here searching."

"You did?" Her voice broke at the revelation.

He nodded. "Then in October 2015, I went to Buffalo to search and pass out flyers. By then, it had been ten months since you disappeared, and people were heartless to me. They said to give up, you were dead. I just walked away from them." A tear slid from his cheek. "How can people be so sick? To tell a desperate man that his fiancée was probably dead and to give up? I can't imagine telling anyone that. I couldn't give up though."

Bethany suddenly snuggled up in his arms, silently crying into his arms.

Lucas gladly wrapped his arms around her, and he could smell the pomegranate-scent shampoo coming from her hair. It was intoxicating.

"In February 2016, I went back to New York City for a week. I just did the same thing, passed out flyers and interviewed shop owners. Nothing. No leads at all. April 2016, I went to Albany for a week, but still nothing. In September, I received a call that they found your dead body in a graveyard. You had been murdered."

"WHAT?" Bethany shrieked, in shock that someone said that to him.

"It was a sick joke because when I came to Newburgh, where they said your body was at the morgue, it was all fake. All a joke." Lucas couldn't hide his tears once more. "People thought it was funny to tell me that the person who meant the whole world to me was dead. They thought it was funny to make up a story about it, when, in reality, it just made me want to kill myself. I didn't care about my fame or fortune. I just wanted to join you, but I found out when I visited the morgue in Newburgh that it was all a joke. I was relieved but devastated. I didn't know where else to search."

Bethany tried to contain her sobs. "I'm so sorry you went through that."

"I felt my heart shattered when I heard the voice tell me that you were murdered." Lucas had more than a few tears now. He didn't bother wiping them away. He let himself be vulnerable to her. "I just wanted to hold you in my arms and keep you safe, to let you know I was there and I had found you. I wanted you to be back home so your parents could say goodbye and I could visit you daily, but it wasn't you."

"Does a part of you wish it was me?" Bethany asked carefully.

Lucas closed his eyes and held her even closer to his bruised and battered body. "You have to look at it from my point of view though, Beth. I didn't know what the hell was happening to you. I hadn't had a decent night of a sleep because the nightmares of you being used for sex, tortured, raped, or trapped were always clouding the positivity of my mind . . . My heart wrenched every single day not knowing if you were safe and sound, if someone was abusing you daily." He let his sobs be released. "I just wanted to know where you were!"

Bethany took this time to comfort him like he did for her twice already that day. "Oh, Lucas, I'm so sorry."

"You have no idea how it feels to have you in my arms right now!" he said loudly, sobbing into her hair. "I'm so glad it wasn't you though! I am so happy and thankful to God that it wasn't you! I haven't come back since then because it was just too painful to keep going back onto that plane empty-handed! But I kept paying my private investigator because I was not giving up on you!"

"And now you're here, baby," she whispered in his ear. "You're here. You found me."

"I'm so thankful." Lucas softened his tone as he kept his grip on her. "I don't want to leave you ever again. Can't you understand now? I don't care about my career, I don't care about my place over there, I don't care about anything. I just want to be with you. The entertainment and fame have no value to me, just being here with you today has meant so much to me. I love you so much."

"Sweetheart . . ." Bethany sighed. "I still love you too. I never stopped. I still wear the engagement ring you gave me, but I think your career has been so amazing. You shouldn't give it up for me."

"Bethany," Lucas groaned.

"Okay, how about this . . ." Bethany smiled. "Do the show and then see how you feel after the show."

"Will you go back with me for a little bit?" Lucas asked in hope.

Bethany raised her eyebrows and then giggled. "I walked right into that one."

"Look, I'll do the show, but please come back with me, come watch the show. Visit your parents. Maybe get some inspiration for a new book? But please, I can't be separated from you again," Lucas pleaded.

Bethany sighed deeply. "Is that the deal you're offering?"

Lucas laughed. "Yup. Take it or leave it. Either you come back with me so I can do the show and then we move me over here forever . . . or you can stay here, and I'll stay here too, quitting the show." He shrugged with a smirk. "Either way, we are stuck like glue."

Bethany rolled her eyes and threw her hands up in the air in exasperation. "Fine! You win! I'll come to Hollywood for a little while, but then we return here afterward."

"Deal!" Lucas suddenly became bold and grabbed her face, letting his lips softly crush her lips.

Bethany seemed shocked but kissed him back.

Lucas walked Bethany up to the doorway of her large house. "You have a nice house," he commented, not being able to look her in the eyes.

Bethany smiled. "Thank you. Well, I better go inside."

"Do you . . . um . . . would you . . . I mean, you don't have to . . . but do you . . ." Lucas mentally smacked himself. Speak up!

Bethany giggled and stepped closer to him. "Are you asking me out, Mr. Law?"

Lucas sighed in relief since, apparently, he couldn't ask her in a mature way. "Yes."

"I'd love to." Bethany poked his chest flirtatiously. "What about tomorrow?"

"Perfect," Lucas said, feeling his heart flutter. "Can I pick you up around five?"

"Sounds wonderful." Bethany then stepped a bit closer to him, and he felt his breath leave his body. "I had an amazing time with you tonight," she said softly.

He could smell her perfume since she was so close.

Could he do this? He needs to kiss her! Why wasn't he moving?

"Um . . . yeah . . . I had loads of fun," Lucas stuttered out. "Ditching the dance and eating at a diner? Simple . . . but totally fun . . . My favorite."

"Mine too." She blushed. Realizing he wasn't going to kiss her, she felt a little let down. "Well, I guess this is good night."

Lucas went to leave as she opened the door, but he couldn't; he suddenly grabbed her wrist before she could go inside and yanked her back to him. She stumbled and fell onto his chest, but he caught her with ease. Before he could overthink anything, he quickly pressed his lips onto hers, giving the girl he had just met hours before his very first kiss.

She kissed back with passion.

Lucas swore this moment came from a fairytale.

Lucas loved that memory as he released the kiss they shared for the first time in so many years. Bethany looked very happy.

Lucas rubbed his lips together before speaking. "I just want you to know that I haven't been with anyone since you. I haven't even kissed another woman since you."

Bethany smiled and touched his face with her gentle touch. "Me neither. I couldn't imagine ever being with someone else other than you."

Lucas suddenly was a bit nervous as he put his hands on her waist. "So no man has touched you?" He pleaded with her to answer him as she maneuvered herself on his lap, straddling him.

Bethany wrapped her arms loosely around his neck, looking seductively at him. "Nope. I'm still untainted. All yours."

"Oh god, yes."

Lucas let out a breath he didn't even know he was holding in as they kissed once more with even more passion than before.

Soon he maneuvered down to her neck and collarbone, let her moan at his touch. "Are you . . . ah!" He pressed his lips down at a sensitive spot. "Are you . . . positive . . . you're . . . not . . . sore?"

"Oh, I'm sore as hell," Lucas growled in a husky tone as he pulled at her shirt in effort to remove it. "I just don't care right now."

"I've missed you," Bethany said breathlessly as they passionately kissed once more.

CHAPTER FOUR

Failure

June 4, 2017

After finishing dressing herself so she could leave for her appointment in a timely fashion, Bethany stepped out of her bedroom and went to check on her fiancé.

He had been up early this morning.

She blushed remembering their first night together since they were twenty-two years old, still amazing as it was almost three years ago.

Bethany walked into the large kitchen and saw Lucas leaning against the kitchen counter, teasing Loki with a piece of bacon.

She rolled her eyes. "Lucas Simon Law, don't you dare give him that piece of pig slaughter!"

Lucas was startled, not realizing she was there, but then grinned. "Still hate how pigs are sacrificed for this delicious meal?" he said as he put the piece in his mouth.

"It's cruel," Bethany told him as she realized he made breakfast. "Well, well, someone woke up very happy today."

"Very, very, oh so very happy," Lucas told her as he strained himself to walk to her and kiss her lips. "Last night was amazing."

"Where is your cane?" she asked him.

Lucas rolled his eyes. "It's been about eighteen hours since the accident, and I feel better already. Isn't there a saying somewhere that great lovemaking makes everything better?"

She didn't answer him as she pecked his lips a second time and then grabbed some breakfast. "So what are you so dressed up for?" she asked as they both sat down to eat at the breakfast nook next to the large window that looked down at the busy packed streets. "That outfit is adorable but a little overdressed for bedrest."

Lucas chuckled. "Well, I was hoping I could go with you to your appointment."

Bethany quickly shook her head. "Nope. You need your rest if you're going to be ready for your show in a few weeks."

"Bethany, come on. I'll rest when we get back, please," Lucas pleaded. "I just want to make sure everything is okay with you."

"It's just my lupus acting up again, babe," Bethany told him, trying to sustain his worries.

"Lupus is serious, no matter how much you try to tell yourself that it's not." Lucas sighed. "Please, let me come."

"Nope, nope, and nope." Bethany checked her small watch and stood up suddenly. "I have to head out. It's an hour until my appointment, and I need to be on time."

Lucas just stayed silent as he was pouting.

Bethany giggled as she pecked his cheek. "I'll be back, my love."

Lucas turned his head to her and smirked. "I love you, meanie."

Bethany blew him a kiss as she grabbed her purse and went into the elevator, closing the doors and pressing the down button.

She winced in pain as her back was having sharp pains.

She almost collapsed but leaned on the nearest wall of the elevator.

She almost wished she had taken Lucas up on his offer to go with her.

... ...

"We've done all the tests possible."

"Looks like the lupus has done its worst."

"We need to start you in dialysis as soon as tomorrow."

"This is stage 4 of your kidney failure. We have to work fast."

"You may need to let your family and fiancé know now . . . just in case."

Bethany fiddled with her engagement ring and wedding band that she still hadn't taken off as she sat outside her building, wondering how to tell her fiancé, who spent almost three years searching for her, that her kidneys have failed.

She may die.

Now she had to dialysis three times a week, so she couldn't possibly go to California with him.

Why was this happening?

Whenever Bethany was scared like this, she only knew one person to call: the woman she hadn't talked to since the attack on her and her stillborn child.

Ring. Ring. Ring. Ring.

"Hello?" the voice on the other end of the receiver sounded so tired.

Bethany almost instantly broke down at the sound of her mother's voice. Oh, why did she disappear for so long? Her mother sounded so lonely and sad.

"Mommy?" she whimpered on the phone. "I need help."

"Bethany?"

Bethany sniffled against her tears. "Yes, Mommy, it's me."

"Oh, my sweet daughter, how I've missed hearing your beautiful voice." Her mother sounded to be crying as well. "Tell Mommy what's going on."

"I'm sure you've seen the news and papers that Lucas found me." Bethany started the devastating explanation. "It's been amazing, and we're back together, not that we ever weren't, but this time it's forever."

"I'm so glad. You two were always so good together."

"But, Mom, I just left my nephrologist, and he said my lupus took a toll on my kidneys, and now I'm in stage 4 kidney failure." Bethany tried to wipe her tears. "I've been trying to keep myself strong all these years, but nothing is stopping it. It's won. I'm dying. The doctor said he's starting me on dialysis tomorrow for three times a week, but he said that's only going to prolong it. Mom, I'm dying. I'm dying, and my fiancé just . . .

I don't know what to do. I need help." Bethany sobbed out, unable to control herself.

"Oh my god, honey . . ." It sounded as if her mother was out of words, in utter shock of the news.

"I don't know how to tell Lucas." Bethany forced herself to speak, realizing her mom didn't know how to handle this situation. "I just told him last night about the death of our daughter, which he handled fairly well, but this will just break his heart. I don't want to hurt him anymore."

"Bethany, listen to me: Right now, you need Lucas more than ever. I know you want to protect him from the hurt so he can think everything is back to perfection, but you need him. This time, Beth, I refuse to let you shut him out. This is your fiancé, for better or for worse, until death do you part."

"We aren't married yet, so he shouldn't be forced into this." Bethany tried to tell her.

"HE LOVES YOU! What part of that are you not understanding? That man would move heaven and earth to be with you, and guess what? For over two years, he did! You cannot take that away from him! He has every right to be there with you! You need to let him take care of you! That man has been through so much trauma for the past couple of years, so let him run his own life! Quit trying to choose his path for him! He wants to take care of you and protect you! Let him! He deserves that!"

By then, Bethany was crying harshly. "I know, and I will. No matter what he chooses to do, I'll let him."

"Go talk to him, Bethany, please. Now listen, I'm going to talk to your father and Lucas's parents. We'll be there soon. Text me your address in . . . Where in the world have you been hiding?"

Bethany couldn't help but chuckle through her tears. "Manhattan."

"Oh jeez, Lucas went to Manhattan twice! You've always been a sneaky one."

Bethany just smiled. "I love you, Mommy."

"I'm so happy to hear from you . . . I'll be there soon. Give us probably two days."

They hung up soon after that, and Bethany let out a breath that she didn't even know she was holding in.

She mentally prepared herself for the news she was about to deliver to Lucas, but when she stood up to turn to her building, she realized Lucas was behind her, leaning next to her place on the bench behind her.

Tears were streaming down his face.

He knew.

Bethany gulped, waiting for him to say something. She saw Loki next to him.

Lucas had taken him out for a walk; how sweet.

"Please say something," she finally whispered.

Lucas shrugged. "I'm not letting you go without a fight," he simply said, his tears streaming down. He seemed to snap out of it and held out his hand. "Let's go inside."

Bethany decided to not press the subject as she took his hand, and he led both her and Loki back into the building.

As they went up into the elevator, Bethany's mind wandered to the first time they had a scare with her lupus.

Lucas went up the stairs to his girlfriend's bedroom as he had a present for her and some fast food she loved to munch on.

He knew she was sick, and she had gone to the doctor's today, but he was more nervous now. He asked his parents what happened, but they said that Bethany should be the one to tell him.

That alarmed him.

He knocked on her door as he saw her resting in bed, reading a book.

"Hey, beautiful."

She pouted. "I'm not beautiful."

"Why are you wearing a long-sleeved shirt?" he asked, setting her food on her bedside table. "It's summer."

"My rash is ugly," she mumbled.

"Change into a T-shirt, please." He went to her closet and threw her a baggy T-shirt. "Quit being ridiculous." He stayed turned around until she threw her long-sleeved shirt at his head. "Rude," he grumbled as he put the shirt in the hamper. He saw the rash on her arms and winced. "It looks horrible."

"Thanks for rising my self-esteem, jerk." She crossed her arms over her chest, glaring at him.

"I was just stating it looks painful." Lucas smirked as he held up his present. "Besides, don't be mad, I bought you a present and a burger."

"Ooh, okay, I forgive you!" She suddenly cheered as he put the present in front of her. She quickly unwrapped it, and he sat across her on the bed. She opened it and gasped, "Oh, Lucas, you shouldn't have!" She brought out the book that was inside. It was signed on the cover from her favorite author. "SHE SIGNED IT TOO?"

"Yep." Lucas couldn't hold himself up as Bethany hugged him tightly. Her body still felt so hot, it made his stomach drop. "Please tell me what the doctor said."

Bethany sat back. "Oh, it's just lupus."

Lucas's eyes widened. "What the—what do you mean it's 'just lupus'? Bethany, that's serious! We learned about it in health class last year!"

Bethany rolled her eyes as she dug into her food. "Quit being overdramatic, I'll be fine."

"Beth, that can get worse over time." Lucas shook his head in disappointment when he realized she didn't want to acknowledge her illness. It scared him, but he didn't want to upset her. "At least it's summer vacation."

"Yeah, I'll be over this before the semester starts back up," *Bethany told him, eating a french fry. "Dear God, these are* *amazing!"*

Lucas watched her chow down, but in the back of his mind, *he was praying this lupus disease didn't give her a hard time.*

What Lucas didn't realize is that the lupus caused not only symptoms of that disease, but other diseases can also occur because of it. One of them was kidney failure, which is what they've always watched out for.

Apparently, nothing was enough.

From what it sounded like to him, nothing Bethany or the medical team could do to prevent the inevitable.

There had to be a way though.

He was rich. He was wealthy. He had all the money in the world. He didn't need it. He wanted the best doctor to help her. He wanted the best! No matter where he would be coming from, he wanted that doctor.

He wanted to try to do a kidney transplant so he could give her his kidney or even someone else's that matches, but sadly, in stage 4, there's no turning back.

But like he said before, there had to be a way! Life cannot be that cruel that he was going to lose his girl right after he found her!

"I'm going with you tomorrow to dialysis," Lucas told her firmly as she was brushing her teeth before bed that night.

Bethany sighed. "Fine," she said after she spit into the sink.

Lucas sat in the bed, watching Loki lay across the end of the bed. Even in Bethany's large bed, the dog was still longer than the width of it.

"What are the side effects?"

"Babe, why do we have to discuss this?" Bethany said as she turned off the bathroom light and pulled back the covers so she could get in. "I want to have a peaceful night with you."

"I want that too, but you have to understand that I need to fuss over you," Lucas tried to explain to her. "I know you're not used to that, but this is all so sudden to me too."

Bethany smiled as she curled up under the covers with him. "Fine. Fuss away."

"Thank you," Lucas joked as he turned to look her in the eyes as she was still wrapped in his arms. "Side effects?"

"Low blood pressure is a big one," Bethany answered. "I've always have had so many problems with my blood pressure being too low, so we may want to watch for that."

"Okay." Lucas nodded, looking like he was taking in the information. "Now listen, we need to think about our trip to California."

"Lucas, I'll be fine here alone," Bethany told him before he could speak. "You go back for your show, and I'll be here."

"Hmm, let me think long and hard about that." Lucas faked a thinking pose, as if he was really considering letting that happen. "And the answer to that would be *not happening*."

"Oh dear." Bethany sighed. "Please, don't quit your show. If you want, I can try to skip dialysis—"

"That can speed up tragic events, so no, thank you," Lucas told her. "I'm quitting the show, and that's final, Bethany."

Bethany look a little peeved, and she suddenly took his hands off her and turned to get out of the bed. She stepped off the bed and grabbed a pillow. "I'm sleeping on the couch."

"Bethany!" Lucas said, exasperated.

Before an argument can continue, Bethany winced in pain as the shooting pain of her kidneys shot up her back.

She cried out in pain, and Lucas was by her side within seconds. He whispered sweet nothings into her ear as he held her through the painful episode.

He had her go back to bed and adjusted her so she was not keeping pressure on her back with a pillow behind her.

It was then and only then did he realize she was fragile and a breakable porcelain doll.

She needed him more than she knew.

… … … … …

Lucas waited impatiently in the waiting room as they were hooking up his fiancée to the dialysis machine.

Since they needed everyone who wasn't on the dialysis to stay outside, he decided to wait in the waiting room.

He didn't want to be apart from her, but he understood.

While she was being hooked up, Bethany was severely prone to infections.

He was pretty scared to see what was going to be happening. He tried to look it up on the Internet a few hours ago, but it just made him even more scared.

Soon the phone rang, and he saw it was his mom.

"Hey, Mom, it's not a good time."

"Son, is that any way to speak to your mother? I don't think so."

Lucas clenched his fist. "Sorry. What's up?"

"We have our ticket for tonight. We should be there in a couple of days, okay?"

"You guys don't need to come. I can handle this," Lucas said, a little annoyed. "I can take care of my fiancée."

"Oh, honey, we know, but we are all so worried about Bethany, and I haven't seen her in years."

"Fine, but no heart-to-heart talks," Lucas warned. "I'm not listening to reason on this one. I have faith that everything is going to be all right."

"Where's Bethany?"

"Dialysis." Lucas checked the door, but it still remained unopened. "I can't go in and sit with her until everyone in the area is hooked up."

"That's understandable. Well, are you okay, son?"

"I'm fine, Mom. I'm not the one you should be worried about. I'm not the one in agonizing pain." Lucas's voice cracked a little. "Mom, how do I get through this?"

"You just told me that you have faith. Keep it. And give her some faith."

Lucas understood what his mom was saying. "Okay, I will. Thank you, Mom."

"We'll see you in a few days. Take care of her."

His mom sounded like she began to cry by the time they hung up.

Finally, he was allowed to go back to sit with Bethany, who was lying comfortably on a lounging recliner, hooked up to a machine that would be cleaning her blood for the next four hours.

She took his hand, and he gave it a kiss. She seemed so exhausted.

"I'm so drained."

"I bet," he whispered as he gave her hand a squeeze. "What does it feel like?" He motioned to the tube hooked up to the machine that was sticking out of her shoulder.

"I can't really feel anything," she said softly. "I'm so sleepy."

"Sleep, my love," Lucas told her as he kept her hand in his but let his free hand run his fingers through her hair. "I'm here to protect you. I won't let anything harm you."

"Promise?" she whispered. "You won't leave?"

Lucas's lip trembled but kept his emotions intact. "I promise. I'm not going anywhere."

Soon she fell asleep, almost a deep sleep.

For the next four hours, Lucas didn't dare take his eyes off his fiancée.

Everything in the world seemed to go on, but time was currently stopped for him.

He had a few missed calls from Alex, who was very angry. Lucas realized he needed to tell him the truth, but he decided to wait until after he was in the waiting room again.

He couldn't believe the past couple of days.

Just a few days ago, on the second, no one had any idea where Bethany was.

He didn't know if she was okay or even why she disappeared. Then he found her, went to her, and now this; how could life change so quickly? Within three days, his life has done a complete 180.

On the second, he woke up as a spoiled model, the most wanted model in the business. He was getting paid just to wear a certain kind of underwear. He was about to take part in the world's most famous fashion show.

Now he woke up this morning on the fifth, getting ready to take his terminally-ill fiancée to dialysis, not worrying about the soreness and bruises on his body from being hit by a car.

It all seemed to be fading quicker than before because of his determination to take care of his beloved girl.

Life works in mysterious ways.

God is the one who works in strange ways.

The four hours seemed to pass by quickly, and before he knew it, he was asked to step back out to the waiting room while they unhook Bethany from the machine.

As he stepped out, he took out his phone to make that tragic phone call.

"LUCAS! Where the bloody hell are you? I have everyone screaming at me to get you back here to Hollywood! Dude, everyone seen the news about you getting hit by a car just to see your long-lost fiancée! They're pissed! Jim Yang is pissed! Get back over here and save your reputation because everyone thinks you're insane!" Alex seemed a bit on the edge today.

Lucas took a deep breath before continuing, "I quit, Alex."

"WHAT?"

"I quit. I quit the show, I quit modeling, and I quit show business." Lucas sighed. "I've had a good time the past three years, but it's time for me to get my priorities straight."

"Lucas, you're throwing your entire career away for a homewrecker that left you! What is wrong with you? She's obviously with you for the money!"

"Bethany is very sick, Alex. She's in stage 4 of kidney failure because of complications from her lupus disease," Lucas told him bluntly, attempting to not hang up. "She's . . . she's terminally ill."

"Aw, man, I'm so sorry, but, dude, if that's true, then you shouldn't give up your career for someone who's dying."

Lucas wasn't shocked at all by Alex's statement. It's the modeling business.

Everyone was heartless.

"Thanks for your so wonderful sympathy," Lucas said with sarcasm. "Anyways, bottom line: I quit. I'm choosing my fiancée over modeling."

"Dude, come on! These people are planning on paying you so big when you just walk down this stupid runaway at the show! Just come home, do the show, get paid, and then quit!"

"What if something were to happen while I was gone?" Lucas asked. "I'm sorry, but I can't do that. I'm done with Hollywood, and I'm never going back."

"SHE IS NOT WORTH IT, MAN! Don't do this! You're the most wanted man in America! Don't do this!"

"Bethany is worth everything and more." And with that, Lucas hung up the phone and put it away.

He couldn't believe Alex was that heartless, but he again had to remember it was show business. That's how people were when they didn't get their way.

Soon the door to the back opened, and he saw his tiny fiancée walking out with her duffel bag, with her blanket and pillow inside. He immediately took the bag from her so he could carry it and wrapped an arm around her waist.

"Come on, sweetheart," he said as he gently helped her out of the building. "I texted for a driver to pick us up in a few minutes."

"Okay." She sighed as he sat her on the bench in the front. "I feel so nauseous."

"I'm sure," he said as he sat down with her, putting an arm around her shoulders. "We'll be home soon."

"I have so much I need to do," Bethany whimpered. "I need to go grocery shopping for our parents' arrival, I need to clean, I need to give Loki a bath, I need to—"

"Stop," Lucas whispered as he kissed the side of her head in an attempt to calm her. "I'll do all that."

"You don't know how to do any of that," Bethany told him. "Also, aren't you the one who needs rest? You were just hit by a car a couple days ago."

"True, but never a better time to learn, and I'm fine. I'm honestly feeling better already," he told her, realizing she was cold, so he took off his light sweater and wrapped it around her shoulders. "I need you to just rest. I don't care where you rest—your bed, the couches, or even on the balcony. You need to rest."

"I wish I could take a bath," Bethany mumbled. "But they said no baths or long showers with this tube on me."

Lucas sighed, feeling helpless. She was miserable, but he didn't know how to comfort her. "You're still beautiful."

"Liar." She pouted, but Lucas ignored her as he pecked her on the lips. "Stop making me happy. I want to be sad right now."

Lucas chuckled. "Nope. No sadness on my watch." He pecked her lips again, making her giggle. "I love you."

"I love you too." Bethany smiled. "I'm glad you're here. It's strange, isn't it?"

Lucas kissed her head. "What is?"

"You found me when I needed you the most."

CHAPTER FIVE

Shattered

June 6, 2017

Every time Lucas looked at the clock, the time passing by was too slow as Bethany's second dialysis appointment was going painful.

Her leg muscles kept cramping up, so the nurses had to keep adjusting the machine levels. Either the blood was flowing too fast or too slow, or she was taking in too many fluids or not enough. Nothing kept working for Bethany.

They were three and a half hours in, and Bethany was having another cramp, but this time in her stomach. A fever began to form, and her blood pressure took a drop.

After one male nurse put a cold compress on her forehead, he sighed, looking at the machine again.

As she tightened her grip on Lucas's hand, Bethany whimpered, "Why won't this work?"

"People who develop kidney failure from lupus often get resistive to all forms of treatment," the male nurse with a name tag that read "Milo" on it told her with sympathy. "We're going to keep trying, okay? If you don't stop trying, then we won't."

"I won't," Bethany told him in a soft voice. "Please don't give up on me."

The fear and sadness in her voice made Lucas's heart shatter.

Milo reached over and patted her good shoulder that didn't have the tubing in it. "I'm refusing to give up on you, Bethany. I've read all your books, and you've helped me out of some very dark times in my life. This is a miracle to be helping you. You saved my life, and I'm not going to stop working to help you."

Lucas sighed. He really needed to read Bethany's books.

After Milo left her area, Bethany stared up at the ceiling, looking to be praying silently to herself.

Why couldn't he do something to help?

He was useless to her!

"I named her Anastasia." Lucas suddenly heard Bethany speak, and his head shot up to see tears streaming down her face as she played with his hand. He saw her curled up into the large chair, making her look so fragile. "Our daughter . . . Anastasia Rose Law."

Lucas smiled gently. "That's a gorgeous name."

"I thought so." Bethany smiled to herself, not able to look him in the eyes. "She was beautiful. She had thick hair like me . . . your nose . . . my lips . . . your ears . . . She was perfect. Long eyelashes, four pounds two ounces, seventeen inches long. She was the most perfect little person I had ever laid my eyes on."

"What color was her hair?"

"Strawberry blond." Bethany giggled. "She had my hair, but she still looked like her daddy."

"She was a mixture of us both, and she sounds like a beauty queen, like her mother." Lucas leaned up and kissed her temple. "I think we could've made pretty cool parents."

Bethany let out a chuckle. "I think we would've been a mess!"

"Well, there's that too." Lucas laughed. "I honestly do think we were a great team. Still are."

Their laughter died down as everyone else around them kept moving and going about their business, not paying attention to their little bubble. As Bethany had another cramp in her stomach, Lucas began to get that useless feeling back in the pit of his stomach. It was almost burning.

"Uh-oh!" She suddenly shrieked and grabbed the plastic bags on the other side of the chair from Lucas and opened it quickly, just before the vomit heaved out of her. Her body was shaking with a cold sweat, and her stomach was emptying itself violently.

Milo came back over and checked Bethany's vitals again, as Lucas rubbed her back and the back of her neck, trying to ease her violent trembling.

When she was done, Milo handed her a trash can, where she dumped the bag of vomit in, and then Lucas didn't care if she was a mess as he motioned for her to hug him. He held her tightly, wishing he could take this all away from her.

She was sobbing into his shirt. "I don't want to die," she whimpered out in a pitiful voice.

Lucas had to hide his tears from her.

Why was this happening?

After he was led to the waiting area so they could unhook Bethany from the machine, someone suddenly called his name. He looked up and saw a young woman standing in a business outfit, motioning for him to follow her toward the offices in the back.

He immediately followed her, and she led him to her cubicle that read Social Services.

"Have a seat, Mr. Law," the blond woman said as she sat behind her desk.

Lucas did as he was told and sat in an uncomfortable chair across her. She sighed as she clicked a few keys on her computer.

"What is this about?"

"My name is Ginger Benson, I'm the social services designee here at the dialysis center," Ginger introduced herself. "And I'm going to run a few things with you regarding your fiancée's health."

Lucas gulped, worried about the outcome of this conversation. "You don't believe in her, do you? You're giving up on her?"

Ginger shook her head. "On the contrary, Mr. Law, I'm trying to assist her so she can be more comfortable. I have a nurse that has volunteered himself to assist you three days a week in your home you share with Bethany."

"You mean do dialysis at home?" Lucas asked in interest. "She would love that."

"Her insurance covers it, and don't worry, there's a myth about pets cannot be near a dialysis machine. That's not true," Ginger told him. "I know Bethany has a Great Dane as I read in one of her books' profile. He's safe. As long as he's trained enough to stay away from the machine. If I know dogs like that, they're lazy, he won't move."

"When can we start this?" Lucas asked, not really worried about Bethany's monster dog.

"Immediately. Most likely on Friday," Ginger answered. "With people like Bethany, we want to keep them comfortable . . . because she is in the last stage of kidney failure. She needs all the safety measures she possibly can. In here, the building is riddled with infections and sicknesses, though some of our patients can be careful. Bethany's blood results came back, and her levels are low. Her immune system is nonexistent. If she is exposed here at the facility, it could kill her or quicken her terminal illness. We have to take every measure possible."

Lucas nodded, not able to speak.

They want to do this because they are 100 percent positive that Bethany was going to die.

Why didn't anyone believe in them?

"I don't agree," Lucas said suddenly. "She's going to be fine."

Ginger sighed deeply. "Mr. Law, it's not healthy for you to deny what's happening around you."

"You know I just found Bethany again, right?" Lucas asked her.

"I know the whole story since I watch the news," Ginger told him. "That doesn't give you an excuse to live in a world that no bad things happen when something bad is happening right now, Lucas. Bethany needs you to be strong for her, but if you just deny everything, it's going to hurt both of you, especially you."

"I can't go through this again," Lucas said sharply. "I accept your company's help regarding doing the treatments at home."

Ginger shook her head, realizing she wasn't going to change Lucas's mind back to reality. "Fine. I'll call you tomorrow regarding what time he'll be there."

Lucas nodded and immediately left, going back out to the waiting room, where he saw Bethany sitting limply on the chair. Her duffel bag was in the chair next to her, and she had her large jacket over her as she stared at the floor.

Lucas carefully walked up to her and leaned down in front of her, setting his hands on her knees.

"How's my sweetheart?"

Bethany looked defeated. "Lucas, I'm going to die, aren't I?"

Lucas closed his eyes, trying to regulate his breathing. "I told you, I won't let you go without a fight."

Bethany finally looked him in the eyes. "You can't fight something like this. You told me that."

The beeping went through the hospital room while Bethany rested on her side, holding Lucas's hand. She had fainted in psychology class that she had with him, so he went with her in the ambulance. The blood work was being done as they speak.

"I'd rather be bored in my Algebra 2 class than be in here," Bethany said while Lucas sat in the chair next to her bed. "When can I go home?"

"Whenever the tests come back," Lucas said, sounding distracted as he was on his phone. "You know, I've been doing some research on lupus, and it says that there's a lot of different ways it can affect your health."

"I don't want to discuss this," Bethany warned him.

"Just hear me out," Lucas pleaded. When she rolled her eyes but didn't speak, he took that as an "okay" to keep

going. *"Lupus can cause kidney problems, affect the brain and your nervous system, blood issues, blood clots, and having lots of problems in your lungs. Not to mention it's high risk to heart problems."*

"And this is why people always say not to look up stuff on the Internet," Bethany said suddenly. *"You think way too much into it."*

Lucas looked upset as he turned off his phone and stuffed it in his pocket. "Fine, whatever. Don't care about your health. Just let yourself die. See if I care."

Bethany's eyes widened at that last statement.

Lucas sighed, realizing his words. "I'm sorry, I'm so sorry." He took her hand again. *"I'm just so frustrated that you're not taking this seriously."*

"I can fight lupus, okay?" Bethany tried to reassure him. *"I'm not going to die."*

"Babe, sometimes there are some things you can't fight," Lucas told her. *"I'm worried about you. Lupus has no cure, and I don't want to lose you. I wish you would take this seriously. I understand you think you can fight anything that stands in your way, but this is something you can't fight."*

Bethany sighed. "Fine. I'm sorry. I'll take it seriously."

"That's all I ask," Lucas said.

She looked at him. "Would you really not care if I died?"

"Of course, I would." Lucas leaned down and kissed her cheek. *"I would be so devastated. To be honest, I'd want to follow you."*

"Well, don't do that." Bethany grinned. *"If it makes you feel better, I'll just haunt you."*

Lucas laughed. "Sounds like a plan."

Lucas leaned against the kitchen counter as he waited for the hot water to boil in the tea kettle. He had on a regular T-shirt, jeans, and a flannel shirt on top. He couldn't remember the last time he wore such casual clothes. He always had to wear name brand stuff, but he felt so comfortable like this.

As he remembered the day he begged Bethany to realize her lupus could honestly kill her, he realized he lost his faith.

Could he really let her go?

After going through heaven and hell to get her back, could he really have the audacity to let her die in his arms?

He didn't think he could take that kind of tragedy.

Oh, what he wouldn't give to be in her place. He would rather have her bury him than the other way around.

Buzz!

Lucas stood up straight to go talk into the buzzer, hoping it didn't wake up Bethany from her slumber in her room.

"Hello?" he said after pressing the red button to speak.

"Lucas, it's your parents and Bethany's parents, let us in!" his mother said, sounding absolutely exhausted. He couldn't blame her.

Although they were only in their late forties, early fifties, their parents weren't made to fly airplanes for eight to ten hours with lots of layovers.

He pressed the OPEN button next to the speaker button, letting the doorman know it was okay to send their parents up.

He made sure everything was perfect.

He cleaned every single part of the loft, he ordered the groceries from a nearby store, and he even gave that giant dog a bath, which was a workout in itself.

He didn't want anything to stress Bethany out.

As the elevator came up, Lucas helped them open the elevator door to let them in.

"Hey, guys," he greeted in a tired tone, holding it open as they carried their luggage in. He made sure nothing was left in the elevator before closing it. "Was the trip that bad?" he asked, motioning to their fatigued statures and dark circles under their eyes.

"Don't mind us," his mother, Suzanne, said as she took off her coat. "Even in the beginning of June, it's still a bit chilly here."

"Yeah." Lucas nodded as he took their coats and hung them up on the coat hooks against the wall. "Make yourselves at home. I'm warming up water for tea. Bethany is asleep in bed with the dog."

"Oh, she has a dog now?" Bethany's mother, Margaret, said with interest. "How sweet."

Lucas scoffed, "If you like horse-sized dogs."

"How are you holding up, son?" his father, Richard, asked.

Lucas shrugged. "Barely hanging in there."

Bethany's father, George, patted Lucas on the back. "Son, I have to say I can't believe how selfless you are with all this, taking care of her when she needs you. You're a true man."

"Thank you, sir." Lucas gave him a nod. "You look well."

"Thank you. I'm sorry I have to be so honest, son, you look like hell," George told him. "Are you sleeping at all?"

"Nope." Lucas sighed. "I can't. Every time I try, I wake up an hour later after having a nightmare, and I have to check if Bethany is still breathing."

"I just cannot believe this is happening. It's so sudden, but in a way, it's not," Margaret stated. "Lupus has been sneaking up on her since she was eighteen years old. Doctors kept warning her that it can take years or months, or God only knows how long, but lupus was no disease to ignore."

Suzanne frowned. "It's not fair. Lucas just found her after all these years, and now she has to go through this."

"Let's hope the pain isn't too unbearable," Richard said.

George sighed. "Has anyone brought up hospice yet, Lucas?"

Lucas sharply looked at him with disgust. "Excuse me?"

Margret groaned, "George, couldn't you wait until we all sat down and discussed it with him?"

"Discuss what?" Lucas almost growled. "She's not at that point yet!"

"So you want to seriously look me in the eyes and tell me my daughter has responded to the dialysis treatment?" George said roughly. "She's a small girl, Lucas. She has no strength left in her. Lupus has taken everything out of her for so long. How the hell do you expect her to fight this?"

"Do you want her dead?" Lucas asked. "Is that what I'm hearing?"

"Of course not!" George bellowed. "I just don't want my only child to suffer in pain!"

"Okay, okay, that's enough, both of you." Richard stepped in between the two males. "George, let us talk to Lucas. Why don't you and Margaret go visit with Bethany?"

Margaret nodded. "Sounds like a good idea," she said hastily as she pulled on George's arm, who sighed deeply, walking into the hallway.

Suddenly, a screeching came from the kitchen.

"I'll get the hot water," Suzanne said as she rushed over to the kitchen area. Soon the noise stopped.

Lucas ignored his father as he walked out to the balcony, where he seemed to find peace lately. Unfortunately for him, his father came after him and closed the sliding glass door.

"I don't want to talk, Dad," he said as he leaned over the railing. "I said no heart-to-hearts."

"Well, I do want to talk." His father came up and leaned over the railing with him, their elbows touching as the cold wind hit their bodies. "Lucas, you can't argue with Bethany's father like that. You know he has a point."

"So you want Bethany dead too?" Lucas sneered. "Great. Now I have to protect her from both our fathers. Was Mom in on this? Maybe Mrs. Johnson?"

"Stop it, okay?" Richard said sharply. "You know I've adored Bethany since the day you brought her home when you were sixteen years old for us to meet. Remember, you told me after dinner that you were going to be with that girl forever. She became a daughter to me."

"Then why aren't you fighting for her? Why won't anyone else but me fight for her?" Lucas asked him desperately. "I won't give up on her, Dad."

Richard sighed as he tried to figure out what to say. "Lucas, I need you to be honest with me. How much pain is she in?"

Lucas groaned, realizing this was the worst question in the world. "Severe pain, why?"

"I am not against you, nor am I against Bethany, but, son, if you don't help her through this transition, she's going to continue to fight for you," Richard told him.

"Why is fighting for me such a bad thing?" Lucas asked.

"Because the more she fights for you, the more pain she'll be in." Richard's words struck a chord with Lucas. "You and I both know that her body is failing fast, and it's only a matter of time, Lucas. People don't get better from lupus. They gradually get worse until, finally, their body gives out."

Lucas gulped, trying to take in everything. "Her body is giving out, isn't it?"

"I think it already has," Richard told him, patting his shoulder in a feeble attempt of comfort. "I just don't think you're letting her show her true feelings. I think she's hiding her true pain from you so you don't have to see it."

Lucas then broke down, putting his head in his hands. "I can't be strong, Dad!"

"You need to be strong for Bethany." Richard wrapped his arms around his son's head, wishing there was something he could do. "I just cannot fathom what torment you both are going through. I'm so sorry, Lucas."

"I just feel like life is playing this cruel joke on us." Lucas calmed down, but his body was still trembling. "I feel like that life brought us back together after all these years, after so many years of me thinking she was dead or tortured, just to have her slip away from me again. It can't be right!"

"Maybe it's God's way of bringing the both of you back tougher so she wouldn't be alone during this tough time," Richard suggested. "He didn't want her to suffer alone, so He led you to her just in time."

"I'm tired of losing her," Lucas said, his body suddenly feeling exhausted.

His dad had no words for him, so they stayed out there. Just Richard's presence was comforting enough for Lucas in this time of need.

… … … … … …

Lucas went out for a walk later on. Bethany was spending much needed quality time with both sets of parents, so Lucas took that as a moment to get some fresh air. They all understood.

He had been taking care of Bethany for days, and before then, he had been so sore from being hit by the limo. The week he had was probably the roughest so far.

Although Bethany's body was the one shutting down, he felt his was as well.

He knew his phone was still being blown up by Alex.

Why couldn't the world understand he wanted to be alone? For maybe an hour or two, he just wanted to be left alone.

Even outside in busy New York, he wore a scarf and hat with fake prescription glasses to hide his real identity.

Suddenly, loud bells rang in Lucas's ears. He looked up and saw the church before him.

He didn't know it, but his feet were moving again and moving into the church doors. He went past the foyer and saw candles lit everywhere.

There's a cross in the middle of the altar.

He never found himself very religious, but Bethany was. Both sets of parents were religious.

Lucas and God never really found each other though. Maybe now would be a great time than ever. He didn't know what to do though.

Lucas decided to just sit in the second row of the pews, waiting; he didn't even know what to wait for, but something in his heart told him to stay seated.

It was only then did he feel someone sit next to him.

"What brings you to the house of God, son?" a gruff voice said in a slow tone.

Lucas didn't dare look. He was too scared to.

"Um . . . Father . . . I'm lost. I need guidance," he stuttered, staring straight toward the cross. For some reason, he couldn't look at the man beside him.

"I see," the voice said. "Can you tell me what's going on?"

"My fiancée is terminally ill, and she's already in severe pain," Lucas started. "Our parents are already trying to discuss hospice. My fiancée said she'll leave it up to me to decide, but how could I possibly decide such a thing?"

"Hmm." The Father nodded. "I see."

"She's in so much pain," Lucas whispered.

"Son, I think it's almost near impossible to just give God the one you love so much. It's the right thing to do, but it's also the worst feeling in the world. It's like saying, 'You made this maiden to be my soulmate, but then you want to take her from me' kind of scenarios."

Lucas bit his bottom lip. "I can't let her go."

"What does she have, son?"

"She was diagnosed with lupus at the age of eighteen. Since then, she's had her share of medical problems," Lucas answered. "Now she's in stage 4 of kidney failure, and there's no going back. It takes everything in her to sit through a four-hour dialysis treatment."

"Hmm." The Father sighed. "She's not responding to any treatment?"

"No. She did from age eighteen to now, but suddenly, everything is failing her so fast." Lucas put his face in his hands. "The doctors have tried everything to slow the progression down, but nothing will stop it."

"I see. Son, you need prayer."

Lucas shook his head. "I don't know how to pray, Father. My fiancée and my parents have always been the religious ones. I never was able to get that bond with God like they did."

"You know, there couldn't be a better time to start creating that bond than right now when you need God the most in your life." The Father tried to comfort Lucas. "There's so much to prayer for in these dark times. The world is under attack by the devil: terrorist attacks, murders, rapes, theft, kidnappings, and more. Sometimes people often forget that God is also watching out for our situations. But He cannot help us until we ask for help."

Lucas rubbed his lips together. "Can you help me?"

"Of course, son." The Father patted Lucas on the shoulder. "What's your fiancée's name?"

"Bethany."

"And yours?"

"Lucas," he answered, almost getting a chill down his spine. He could swear that there was another presence sitting here with them, and the energy was intense.

"Dear God Almighty in heaven," the Father suddenly started speaking loudly, keeping one hand firmly on Lucas's shoulder and the other hand lifted into the air. "Give us grace, oh Heavenly Father. You are in our hearts. You know what is in our minds. You know how we need You dearly, Jesus."

Lucas listened intensely. He closed his eyes, leaning over his knees, almost curling up.

"Bethany . . . young, young Bethany . . . She's hurting, my Lord. She's in pain. Father, we don't care what she has because we know there is no illness or disease too strong that You can't handle. No matter what Bethany has, she is well aware that You are in control."

Lucas felt the tears leave his eyes and his body trembling.

"Help Bethany, Jesus. Help Lucas. Help them both become a stronger couple in You, Father. And please, help them face these trials as a power team. Please help them realize not to tell You how big their storms are . . . but to tell the storm how big their God is. You, Father, are their God Almighty."

That sent more chills down his spine.

"God, may Your will be done."

....

As Lucas walked down the street toward Bethany's loft, his phone vibrated. He checked it to make sure it wasn't Bethany but saw Alex across the screen.

It was a message.

Text Message from Alex: *I'm flying over to Manhattan. I need to discuss this with you. I feel like you are blinded by dreams, and I have to show you the reality around you! I'll be there tomorrow. I have Bethany's address already because I tracked your phone.*

Lucas rolled his eyes as he put the phone back in his pocket. "Of course. More drama. I need some more in my life right about now, especially when life is falling apart," he grumbled to himself.

It was dark out, and he could see his breath, realizing how much the temperature had dropped in the past couple of hours.

Suddenly, someone came walking toward him and smiled brightly at him.

Bethany?

Lucas was about to start yelling at her as he stopped in his tracks, letting her walk closer to him, but he realized what would be the point of that?

Yelling at someone who just wanted the pain to go away? That would be heartless.

Bethany made it up to him and stopped directly in front of him as he smiled at her. Her grin was contagious.

"Hey, stranger," she whispered, shivering in the cold.

"Did you get bored?" Lucas asked, wrapping his arms around her and brought her to his chest. The smell of pomegranate was so intoxicating coming from her.

It was hypnotizing.

"As selfish as it sounds, it was a bit crowded at the loft." Bethany sighed, leaning her head on his chest. "I'm not used to having you around, let alone my parents and yours. My home went from just me and Loki, then a week later, it's full of six people and a very big dog!" She giggled. "I sound ungrateful, huh?"

"Nah, not at all," Lucas told her, letting her lean back so he could look her in the eyes. "You were all alone for so long, it's understandable."

"Seeing my mom after so long was amazing though," Bethany told him as he led them to a nearby bench, the same bench she sat on a few days before when he overheard her phone call to her mom. "My dad . . . I don't know, things are weird."

"How so?" Lucas asked her as he sat her on his lap.

Oh, how he missed this.

"He kept bringing up why you won't call some hospice places," Bethany mumbled. "He wants me gone, huh?"

"No, no, no." Lucas leaned his head on her shoulder, struggling with the words. "He loves you so much. He just doesn't want to see you in pain."

Bethany had scared eyes as she looked at Lucas. "You agree with him?"

Lucas's jaw dropped.

Why can't anything go right for him?

He wanted to be respectful to both her father and to his fiancée, of course, but he didn't want to agree with her father. Then again, he didn't want Bethany in pain.

Why was this all put on him?

"Beth . . . are you just fighting for me?" Lucas asked suddenly, letting her process his question.

Bethany stayed silent for a moment before leaving his lap, and she stuck her hands into her coat pockets before walking toward her building.

Lucas stood up and was confused. "Bethany!"

Bethany stopped in her tracks and turned to him sharply, tears of anger streaming down her cheeks. "Yes, I was fighting for *just* you, but I guess that was a mistake. I guess the two most amazing men in my life just think I need to die already. So fine, call hospice," she sneered with bitterness. *"See if I care."*

See if I care.

Lucas was frozen with regrets as Bethany went back into the building.

Those were the exact words he used when they were in college and she was in the hospital because of her lupus.

He thought she had forgiven him, but she never forgot.

He sat back on the bench, sitting in shock of himself and his actions.

And then he came to terms that Bethany took his question the wrong way. Instead of hearing him out, she assumed that he meant that she needs to stop fighting for him because he wanted to move on.

Why couldn't anyone understand him today?

And better yet, why couldn't he voice his feelings?

CHAPTER SIX

Monster

June 7, 2017

One part of today that Lucas could appreciate was the fact that their parents decided to give them some time, and all went out to see a dinner and a movie for a date night.

Lucas felt that he Bethany really needed a night to themselves.

Ever since the night before, where Bethany took his words in the wrong context, he hadn't had the guts to even speak to her about the incident.

Bethany had been in a deep depression. No one could talk her out of her mindset.

She kept saying she was ready to die and to do the hospice.

It just broke Lucas's heart to hear her talk like this.

After their parents left, Lucas walked toward Bethany's balcony, where he was quickly alarmed with her stature.

She was leaned dangerously over the railing, with her feet on the bottom of the bars.

Tears were streaming down her cheeks, and she was shaking violently.

Thank goodness, her glass doors were quiet as he sneaked outside. He silently walked toward her, and she wasn't hearing him at all. He heard her intake a sharp breath and then quickly let out a sob.

There's his chance.

Before she knew what happened, Lucas snaked his arms around her waist and snatched her off the railing before anything else could happen and carried her inside with ease. He set her back on the ground and locked the glass doors behind him.

Bethany glared at him.

"What is your problem? I was just looking!" she screamed at him as she wiped her tears away quickly.

All Lucas could do was turn around and stare at her. He was emotionless. No anger, no sadness. Just emotionless.

Bethany scoffed. "See? You don't even care! Just let me do what I wanted to do in the first place then, if you don't care about me! Obviously, I'm just an annoyance to you! Let me do you a favor so you can hurry off to your modelling career! Don't let me stand in your way!"

Lucas took a deep breath and exhaled.

"Are you done?" he asked in a low tone.

Bethany couldn't believe his heartlessness toward her.

"Why did you come after me if you don't care about me?"

Silence.

When he didn't answer, she shook her head in disgust. "I hate you! Why did you do this to me? Why did you make me fall back in love with you, if you just wanted me gone? Why? I hate you so much! I hate you!"

Still no response.

She stepped up to him and began punching him in the chest with her fist. With his built physique, it didn't bother him at all.

"I hate you! I hate you! I hate you! Go back to Hollywood! Just leave me here to die! I never wanted you to come back in the first place! You didn't see me looking for you! Right? Right?"

No response.

"That's right! I didn't want to know if you still cared about me! Now that you're here and you put my hopes up, it just hurts more! Why did you do this to me? I hate you! I'll never, ever love you again!"

She continued to punch his chest weakly.

Lucas let her tire herself out as she collapsed to the floor.

Soon all the energy had left her as she leaned on his torso, both of them on the floor.

Lucas wrapped his arms around her, feeling how cold she was. He immediately took off his zip-up sweater and wrapped it around her shoulders. It was almost like a small blanket on her.

Careful not to harm the tubing in her shoulder, he put his arm underneath her back and the other underneath her knees. He carried her gently to the one of the recliners and sat her on his lap once he was comfortable. He began rocking her back and forth as she was sobbing into the crook of his neck.

He just didn't know what to say or think.

He wasn't emotionless.

He had quite a bit on his mind. He didn't know how to verbalize them.

Why can't he do it? He had never been good at his feelings, ever.

The year 2010 was finally here! Amazingly, Lucas had a haircut, was now toned up, and lost the glasses so he could replace them with contacts. He went from being the new guy in tenth grade whom no one would go near to now being a senior and one of the popular guys at the school.

Everyone tried to be friends with him.

Girls wanted to be with him.

For seventeen-year-old Lucas, he only had one person on his mind 24/7, who was Bethany.

Bethany hadn't changed much. She was still short, still with her waist-length strawberry-blond hair, and kind personality.

It had been over two years of them being together, and he was head-over-heels for her.

Unfortunately, today he messed up.

They were at a party for the New Year.

One of their drunk so-called friends came up and forced a drunken kiss upon Bethany during the countdown to midnight.

Lucas didn't know what came over him when he yanked her behind him to protect her and punched the guy in the face. The guy fought back, and his friends helped, but Lucas was so overpowered with jealousy and rage that he took them on. Suddenly, everyone feared him.

So did Bethany, who ran out of the party.

As he pulled up to her house at twelve thirty, past midnight, he prayed she would come outside.

Shocking enough, she was waiting for him on the front porch.

She had her legs pulled up to her chest, and her chin was resting on her knees. She still had her black leggings and gray dress sweater on from the party, along with her knee-length black boots. Her hair was half up, half down, and she looked beautiful to him.

Lucas walked up to the front steps and waited for her to acknowledge him before he sat next to her.

They sat in silence for quite a while.

The moon was shining down on them, and crickets could be heard.

Lucas finally cleared his throat. "I'm sorry I scared you."

Bethany turned her head limply toward him. "You really did. I've never seen you like that."

Lucas turned his body toward hers cautiously. "I'm not like that. We've been in a relationship for over two years. I love you. I adore you more than anything in the world."

"I know that's not your true self." Bethany sighed. "What's going to happen when we go to UCLA in the fall? What if we get partnered with different people in a class? Are you going to get jealous and beat him up?"

"Beth, he kissed you," Lucas told her. "I'm not going to be okay with some dude assaulting my girl."

"He was drunk." Bethany shrugged. "He was so wasted that he didn't know."

"I'm never going to be okay with it," Lucas said firmly. "But I do get it. No, I'm not a jealous guy, babe. You know that. I know you're not a jealous person either. I know I have no reason to ever be jealous. You'll never do me wrong."

"Of course not." Bethany smiled, scooting over to him, and he wrapped his arms around her. "I'm so lucky to even be with someone so amazing as you."

"I'm the lucky one." Lucas kissed her forehead. "I love you so much."

Bethany suddenly kissed his lips and smiled against them. "I love you more."

Bethany's sobs settled down to hiccups. Lucas never stopped rocking her. He could feel her body heating up from a fever, and her shivers were still so frequent.

"Bethany . . ." Lucas sighed out, hoping to talk to her about everything that had occurred in the past twenty-four hours.

Suddenly, something stopped them.

BUZZ!

Lucas raised an eyebrow. "Our parents are back early."

"Let them in, please," Bethany mumbled as she slid off his lap when he stood up slowly. "We can talk in my room or something."

Lucas nodded to her as he went toward the buzzer and pressed the button to let them up. He waited for the elevator to come up so he could help open the door. To his shock, someone opened the door for themselves.

When he saw who it was, he knew tonight was going to get worse.

"Alex, this is not the best time!" Lucas snapped suddenly as Alex stepped in and put the door back down after. "Did you not hear me?"

"Yes, I did, and I'm ignoring you." Alex smirked quickly and then sighed, looking toward Bethany, who was standing up to greet him. "Oh, Bethany, how are you? I don't think you remember me—"

Bethany smiled. "Alex. You were in the process of getting Lucas his first modeling audition when I met you last. You've done an amazing job with him."

"Believe it or not, this kid doesn't even need me anymore." Alex patted the back of Lucas, who was glaring at him. "He's so famous, he can say 'I'm running for president,' and he'll win!"

Bethany giggled. "You're such a character."

"Yeah, he's hilarious," Lucas muttered. "Anyways, Alex, what the bloody hell are you doing here? I told you, I quit."

Alex turned back to his friend and rolled his eyes. "Let me explain. Jim Yang is so desperate for you to just *show up* to his fashion show! He is willing to pay you five times the original amount just to have you sit in the front row of his show! You won't even have to do anything!"

Bethany gasped, "Whoa!"

Lucas shrugged. "That number means nothing to me."

"WHAT?" Alex practically had fire in his eyes. He was exasperated as he threw his hands up in the air. "Dude, what will it take? This will be big! You are America's sexiest man alive at this very moment! You are missing out on so many opportunities!"

"He has a point," Bethany spoke up.

Lucas glared to her. "No, Bethany."

Bethany was confused. "Why? I'm dying, Lucas! I don't need you to sacrifice your whole career for me! It'll just be a waste!"

Lucas shook his head in disappointment. "You still don't get it, do you?"

"I don't have to understand anything!" Bethany snapped. "I just don't want you to give up everything you've worked so hard to achieve for some girl who's dying!"

"You're not dying!" Lucas growled back at her. "Last night proved to me that you are not ready to let go! Neither am I! I just wanted you to not be in pain, but I've realized that if you are going to fight to stay alive, no matter what, then I'm going to support you!"

"It doesn't matter if I want to live or not. The fact of the matter is: *I am dying*! I may not be giving up, but my body is giving up! I have nothing left in me to fight for!" Bethany shrieked. "Don't you understand what I'm saying? We can deny and deny all we want, but the reality is that nothing will save me! NOTHING!"

"Shut up!" Lucas shouted at her.

Bethany shook her head. "No! You have to accept that fact! I am dying! Lupus won! Lupus has officially won! We lost! No matter what, we lost, and we aren't going to make a comeback!"

Lucas knew he was going to combust. He turned to Alex, who was grinning at this scene. "Is this entertaining for you or something? Get out!"

Alex lost his grin and sighed. "No, Lucas! I'm with Bethany on this one! This is not the show you can miss! I'm not going to let you throw your entire career away for . . . for . . . for her. Okay, I said it." Although he tried to seem cold, Alex couldn't hide the regret from his words in his eyes.

"You don't mean that," Lucas told him.

Bethany stepped up to Alex. "Please tell Mr. Yang that Lucas will be there."

"You can't decide my life, Bethany!" Lucas yelled at her, making her turn around to face him. "Stop running my life! First, you shut me out and hide from me for almost three years, not letting me be with the woman I adore more than anything in the world! Now you're trying to run me off when you need me most!"

"I just want what's best for you!" Bethany told him, tears leaving her eyes.

"YOU ARE WHAT IS BEST FOR ME!" Lucas shouted in her face.

Suddenly, Bethany's eyes froze into his.

It wasn't a loving stare.

It was almost glossy.

Lucas's heart skipped a beat as her eyes rolled to the back of her head and she fell backward, but both he and

Alex caught her before she could hit the wood floor. Her body began convulsing, and Lucas quickly put her on her side, letting the seizure ride out.

"Call an ambulance, please!" Lucas cried out to Alex.

Alex was frozen but still took out his cell phone, stepping away from the scene.

Lucas let the seizure on, and he took his sleeve to wipe something on the left of her face.

He raised her into his arms and cradled her close to him, wishing none of this was occurring.

She was barely audible, and he couldn't even hear her words. He tried and tried, but nothing made sense.

Her body was still in shock and twitching every other second. Her breathing was uneven and rapid, with her skin pale and clammy. Her fever was higher, and she was shivering from the cold.

It then occurred to Lucas that no matter how much he denied it, or how much Bethany tried to fight, the lupus has won.

However, he wasn't letting Bethany go without a fight, but neither was lupus.

"I'm sorry I couldn't protect you enough, Bethany," he whispered and kissed her forehead. "I've failed you."

… … … … …

Lucas and Alex waited in a private waiting room, considering once they entered the emergency room, everyone wanted Lucas's autograph.

The hospital almost asked if they could leave so there wouldn't be too much commotion, but when Lucas refused, they had no choice but to set them up there.

Alex was almost guilt-ridden.

"I'm sorry I caused this," Alex whispered.

He looked to have startled Lucas, who immediately lifted his head to stare him down.

Alex gulped but continued, "I was selfish. I just thought that maybe if I could save your career, that maybe . . . maybe I could make a better name for myself in Hollywood. I could be the guy who saved Lucas Law from making a huge mistake."

"Bethany isn't a mistake though," Lucas told him. "I've been so loved and happy since I've seen her again."

Alex raised his eyebrows. "How's that? Since you been here, you've found out your fiancée was mugged and assaulted, your first child was stillborn, and now she's dying of kidney failure. Sounds less happy and more tragic."

"Yes, that's all bad." Lucas sighed. "But for the past three years, I've been living in constant fear that something happened to Bethany, that she was being tortured and beaten on an everyday basis, or even that she could've already been dead. My mind was running wild with assumptions."

"So?"

"So, Alex, it has meant the world to me just to know that she's alive and safe," Lucas explained. "Bethany is so amazing. I couldn't imagine a world without her, but I've had to for almost three years, and now . . . and now I might have to again but this time forever."

Alex rubbed his lips together. "I'm sorry for what you're going through, man. And I'm sorry for causing even more heartache."

"It's fine." Lucas shrugged. "The seizure was going to happen. It had been building. Whether it happened tonight or tomorrow, it was going to happen."

Alex nodded and then stood up. "I'm going to head back home now. I have to grovel on my knees once I get there."

Lucas watched him leave. He wondered if Alex would change now.

It began to dawn on him that everyone in the world knew about his engagement with the famous author, Bethany Lou. It was on the cover of every magazine. It was all over the Internet homepages. Even on social media, it was full of rumors.

No one knew about their stillborn child.

No person could ever think that Bethany disappeared from him because of an attack that had no attention.

Everyone thought their engagement was a hoax.

Bethany needed more publicity for her books.

Lucas was tired of being bothered about never having a girlfriend or not coming out as gay.

Society couldn't possibly understand their story.

No one understood that they've been in deep love since he was sixteen and she was fifteen years old.

No one could comprehend that even when they were separated for almost three years, they were still so madly in love with each other.

Lucas swore that there couldn't be a real love like theirs.

And now, look at what's happening. The reality of the situation is Bethany was going to die. It was no one's fault. It was life.

Once he received the okay to go to the private room they set her up in for the time being, he went in and sat next to her as she was staring at him from her spot in the middle of the large bed. She looked so little. The air mattress was practically swallowing her up.

They sat in silence once more.

Finally, Lucas found the ability to speak. He cleared his throat and looked up into her exhausted brown eyes.

"I forgive you, Bethany," he said, straightforward.

Bethany blinked. She didn't seem confused, but she also seemed to wait for him to continue. This obviously was important for him to get off his chest.

"I forgive you for taking away my chance to be with you for the past few years," Lucas continued. "I didn't realize that a small part of me held a grudge against you for that."

Bethany nodded, biting her lip. "It's understandable."

"I do want you to know that even though we were separated, there wasn't a moment where I hated you, and there wasn't a second that I thought you left me for someone else," Lucas told her, taking her hand into his. "No matter what, I always knew that you loved me. I felt it every second of every day in my heart."

Bethany smiled as he kissed her hand. "I love you too, Lucas."

The atmosphere went quiet for a while; it wasn't an awkward silence. It was more peaceful than anything.

"Lucas . . ."

"Yeah?"

Bethany sighed. "Can we go on a trip?"

Lucas was intrigued. He leaned toward her and kissed her cheek, making her smile. "Anywhere you want to go. Sky's the limit."

"Can we go back to Greece?" Bethany whispered. "That month we were there, just the two of us, was the best month of my life."

"That was the month before we discovered your lupus," Lucas muttered in deep thought. "We were on top of the world. No cares in the world."

"I want to go back to that," Bethany told him.

"What about dialysis?" Lucas was terrified of her answer.

Bethany then looked down and let go of his hand.

Lucas gulped, not wanting this conversation to go on, but he had to be strong, and this was the only way. "Would . . ." He swore he had to hold back vomit. "Do . . . I can't believe I am asking this . . . Do you want to . . . stop treatment?" He thought he lost all the color in his face.

Bethany nodded timidly. "Yes, please. I think we should set up hospice over there. There's no place I would rather be when I die than in your arms in Greece. I want Loki there too."

The amount of courage and strength Lucas had to muster up at this moment was unbelievable. No matter how much he wanted to just quit and say "No! You cannot give up!" he knew it was the only way to ensure Bethany's painless end of life.

How could life be this cruel?

He officially hated reality.

"Okay." Lucas nodded. "I'll ask the staff for information. We'll set up a meeting as soon as possible. The moment you're discharged, we will be on the next plane to Greece. I'll even make sure we have the same beach house our parents rented for us years ago. I'm going to make sure everything is . . . is perfect."

Bethany just stared at him with concern and sympathy. Suddenly, she grunted in pain as she tried to sit herself up from the bed. Lucas jumped out of his chair and tried to help her.

She looked back up at him and leaned into his arms. "Lucas . . ."

And that's when he broke down.

The sobs of agony could be heard up and down the halls of the hospital.

He wrapped his arms around her tightly, letting her cry into his chest, and he swore he cried for hours. Every single memory went through his mind that they ever had:

The night they met at the winter formal.

The day he asked her to be his girlfriend.

The day he told her he loved her.

The senior prom in high school when they lost their virginity to each other.

The day they began college.

The trip to Greece.

All her hospital scares from lupus.

The day he was chosen to be a model in a famous magazine.

The day Bethany auditioned for a musical in New York and won the part.

The day he left her in New York to pursue his modeling career and plan their wedding.

The day he never heard from her again until the moment he found her.

The day they became one once more after so long.

The moment he found out he had a daughter who had died because of one man's selfishness to gain a couple of bucks from an eight-month pregnant woman alone walking down the street.

The moment he realized she had to face it all alone.

Now he just had one more milestone left: saying goodbye to her. He was hoping that would happen fifty to sixty years from then, but unfortunately, life was cruel to them.

Eventually, his sobs died down.

Bethany forced her body to scoot over with Lucas's help so he could lie with her in the bed. He wrapped his arms around her tiny figure, embracing the love outpouring from them both.

"Can I make one request?" Lucas whispered in her ear.

"Of course."

"I want to get married before we go."

He needed to do this. He needed to make her his wife. This was exactly what they both needed but mostly him. He needed her to understand how much this meant to him and how much he needed to be able to proudly say he was married to Bethany Lou, the famous author.

Bethany leaned back and smiled brightly through her silent tears.

"I thought you'd never ask."

CHAPTER SEVEN

Marriage

June 10, 2017

Sounds of children playing on the playgrounds in the nearby park rang through Lucas's ears as he was walking Loki. He was hoping to get the large dog some exercise before the plane ride this afternoon. It was around 9:00 a.m., and the wedding was in an hour and a half. All he had to do was take a quick shower, get dressed, and say his "I Dos."

Soon they would be on the plane to Greece, a ten-hour plane ride. Oh joy, how he missed that lovely long flight around the world.

Then again, the last time they took a trip over there, it was a fourteen-hour flight.

He probably shouldn't be complaining about ten hours. He really shouldn't complain at all. He would get all this time with his brand-new wife, and he never wanted anything more.

"AHHH!"

Ow?

Suddenly, two girls, who practically had stars in their eyes, came up to him.

"Oh my god, you're Lucas Law!" one of the girls who had blond hair and blue eyes, almost as tall as him, said in a high-pitched voice.

Lucas winced at the sharpness. "Uh yeah. How's it going?"

"Is this your dog?" the other girl with blond hair too asked, trying to pet Loki, who moved away from her.

"Excuse me, ladies, you are kind of spooking my dog," Lucas grumbled as he tried to maneuver around them.

"Wait, wait, can we have a selfie?" the first girl asked.

"Uh yeah, sure, just be quick." Lucas sighed as they posed for the camera, and he gave a small grin.

"So how are you doing from being hit by that car last week?" one of the girls asked. "You don't seem to be in pain! They said that's why you quit the show!"

"I quit the show because I've quit modeling for my fiancée," Lucas firmly told them. "Now if you excuse me, I have to go. My wedding will be soon."

"WEDDING?" they both shrieked.

Loki groaned at the noise.

Lucas chuckled as he walked away from the girls.

"You know, for a 120-pound dog, you're very sensitive."

And then it dawned on him—who would take care of Loki after Bethany passes?

It's all up to him.

Wait . . . What would happen to everything Bethany has worked so hard to achieve: her books, her dog, her loft, and her career?

Would it all disappear?

Would it all just go away like she never existed?

Lucas realized he couldn't let that happen.

Suddenly, an idea came to him on how to share his wife-to-be's talent with the world.

Lucas smiled to himself.

"Loki, we have quite a bit of work to do."

Loki surprised Lucas with a deep bark, as if he understood.

… … … … … …

Lucas looked aimlessly toward the hall that led to the bedroom door that contained his future wife.

He was so amazed this was even happening to them. If someone would've told him weeks ago that on June 10, he was marrying his fiancée who had been missing for almost three years, then he would've laughed in their face.

He had dreams of this moment. He dreamed of the amazing wedding that would happen.

After a certain amount of time, though, the dream began to become just that: dreams.

They were having the ceremony in the living room.

Both their mothers had decorated a little, and the men had pushed the couches and chairs, along with tables, out of the way into the guest bedroom. There was a preacher there, waiting patiently and praying silently to himself.

Lucas figured he was praying for their marriage, their very short marriage.

There was a narrow red walkway leading from the bedroom to the makeshift altar. There was an arch of flowers where the pastor stood underneath. Flower petals everywhere.

Lucas's father even gave a gift early: He wanted to play the acoustic guitar to "Here Comes the Bride" when Bethany came down the aisle.

It wasn't the wedding they planned all those years ago, but this was definitely exactly what Lucas wanted right now.

He didn't care about the guests, the venue, the groomsmen, the bridesmaids, or the band.

He just wanted to marry the girl he had been with since he was sixteen years old.

After warming up, Richard set down his guitar and came over to his son. He saw Lucas struggling with his bowtie. "Need a hand?" He chuckled.

Lucas let his father take over. "More like six."

"It's a father's duty to help his son with the bowtie anyways," Richard said as he made sure the tie was perfect and smiled. "There you go."

Lucas looked in the mirror and nodded. "Very nice, thank you."

Richard gave a firm nod and cleared his throat. "So . . . I guess this is where I give the father-son talk?"

Lucas scoffed, "Dad, do you know how to give this kind of talk in this situation? Do you have any advice for me on how to take care of my fiancée who's on hospice? Anything to say after the doctor told the girl I love more than anything in the world that she's only going to make it for two weeks? Or how about the fact that the moment we get to Santorini, the hospice nurse will meet us at our beach villa just to explain the process of Bethany dying and how he'll be giving her morphine every couple of hours?"

Richard sighed deeply, feeling so saddened for his son. "No . . . no, I don't have anything like that, but, son, I would love to try."

Lucas looked at his dad, realizing this was affecting him too. He was losing a brand-new daughter-in-law.

"Okay. I'd love to hear it."

Richard looked thankful that he could help in some way. "I'm proud of what you are doing. I would say that you two have not had the fairytale love you wished you could've had, but honestly, you did."

"How's that?" Lucas asked in curiosity.

"Because the story goes like this . . ." Richard took a deep breath and exhaled before continuing, "Boy and girl meet in high school. Boy and girl go to college together. Boy and girl separate to pursue careers. Girl goes missing. Boy never stops searching for her and never gives up hope. Their love goes stronger as they are across the country from each other. Boy finally finds the girl and saves her." Richard patted Lucas on the shoulder. "You saved her. If you hadn't come when you did, she would've been going through all this alone. It's only been a week since you found Bethany again, but you can't tell me you two aren't even more in love than you were when you both were twenty-two years old."

Lucas stayed silent and thought about it. "I didn't think of it like that."

Richard knew his job was done and hugged Lucas in a loving embrace. "I love you, my only child. I'm so proud of you."

Lucas closed his eyes and leaned his head on his dad's shoulder. "I love you too, Dad. Thank you so much."

Richard nodded and left his son standing there to go back to the guitar.

Lucas thought about his words long and hard, and he realized that he had been looking at their situation all wrong.

He came just in time to rescue Bethany; it's like God needed them to be apart before they needed each other the most.

Finally, both mothers came out and were in complete smiles.

Suzanne came up to Lucas. "She's ready."

"Thank you, Mom." Lucas let out a breath of nervousness as his mother went to go stand next to Bethany's.

George went to go to Bethany but suddenly stopped. He turned around and walked up to Lucas, making him look a bit fearful. The men could hardly be in the same room the past couple of days, let alone the same loft. It's been rough, but for Bethany, they'll do it.

Lucas gave a nod of respect to George. "Sir."

George looked tired and worn out as he stood before Lucas. "Son, I just wanted to give my apologies for the way I said things the other day. I know it sounded heartless."

"I've forgiven you, sir, and in a way, I saw your point of view," Lucas told him. "I was in denial, but now I'm seeing things clearly. So in a way, I want to thank you for trying to knock some sense into me."

George nodded. "I didn't want to see Bethany in pain. Margaret talked to me though. She made me realize that Bethany was not our only child, but you are too. You two have been together for so long, and you've never given up on her. I now acknowledge the reality that you are my son too. And I am proud of you. I don't think Bethany could've found someone better."

Lucas gulped, trying to not cry. He had been trying to get George's sincere approval since they were sixteen. The man had always tolerated Lucas being with Bethany, but today he officially accepted him.

"I love your daughter more than anything, and I'll take good care of her," Lucas reassured him.

George gave him a nod and went back to the hallway to get Bethany.

Lucas took another deep breath before walking up to the altar next to the preacher and motioned for his dad to start playing his guitar. Their mothers stood a bit away off to the side, next to Richard.

Soon the door to the bedroom opened, and Lucas swore his stomach dropped and did a hundred flips. This was finally happening, and he prayed it wasn't a dream.

He saw George came out of the hallway, straightening up his tie, looking a bit teary-eyed.

Lucas heard Margaret and his own mom sobbing.

His father's guitar playing sounded angelic and calming.

The butterflies fluttering in his stomach didn't help when Bethany stepped out of the hallway, standing next to her father with a bright smile on her face.

He couldn't believe his eyes. She didn't even look sick!

The tubing for dialysis had been taken out. Now there was only a thin bandage where it was on her shoulder. It was covered by the see-through lace from her dress that covered her collarbones and arms. Her chest down was covered by the lace, but there were sequins, making the gown of white that flowed down to her feet sparkle in the right places. There's a little train behind her of the dress. Her hair was flowing down her shoulders. The veil covered her face, but Lucas could still see her happiness.

It may have not been their dream wedding, but it sure was the wedding Lucas wanted right now.

George led her down the aisle, though it wasn't a long walk since it was just across the living room.

Once they made it to the altar, Lucas had a hard time controlling his calm emotions.

George took Bethany's hand and connected Lucas's with hers, holding them both in his hands. He looked at them both with teary eyes. "Cherish each other. Your love will always last a lifetime, no matter what happens." His voice seemed to crack toward the end of his short speech.

Richard finished his music and put the guitar down to stand next to his wife, who was crying.

The pastor had his Bible in his hands as he looked at the young couple he was about to marry, knowing the circumstances and already being filled in on their story.

"Let's pray."

Everyone put their heads down and closed their eyes.

The pastor sighed deeply, letting his heart speak. "Dear Jesus, we are here to join these two people in Holy Matrimony."

Lucas could hear Bethany sniffle back her tears and gave her petite hands a squeeze for comfort.

"We are joyful in the reunion of these two who have been engaged for three years. No matter how far they were apart, their loved never swayed or withered away. These two are roses that have lived forever. No matter what shall happen within the next few weeks, allow them to know that You are there with them, Lord. In Jesus's name, Amen."

The pastor then opened his Bible to a section the bookmark happened to be and cleared his throat. "The word says, 'For husbands, this means love your wives, just as Christ loved the church. He gave up His life for her,' and I love that verse because it speaks to every couple I marry," the pastor stated, speaking directly to the couple before him. "Beyond the choices you both have made, beyond what is happening right now, and beyond what is going to be happening within near futures, you are doing everything through God. You have both consulted God before making decisions. You have always included God within your love. Whether it'd be Bethany, who's been saved by our Lord since she was a child, or Lucas, who's been saved for a few days, it won't matter to God's eyes.

What matters is how you both have lived your lives from this point forward. What He sees is a husband giving up his entire life to comfort his wife when she needed it the most. That's all that matters."

Now Bethany had tears streaming down her face.

The pastor motioned to Bethany. "You had some vows?"

"Yes." She nodded, keeping her soft grip on Lucas's hands and staring him in the eyes. "Lucas . . . we definitely didn't plan on our magical love story happening this way. We had always dreamed of being famous people and being the most beautiful couple in the world and never breaking apart. And even though there was a huge gap in our relationship of engagement, you never gave up. You never walked away. You kept me close to your heart. For that, I thank you so much. You made me realize that I never should've been apart from you. No matter what, you would've been there for me, and you would've understood everything. Although we do not dwell on the past, if I could go back in time, I would. I would change everything. I would not have been ashamed. I would have been loved and protected by you. Even though our fairytale may not last forever, I'm so glad I've had this week to spend with you, and even though we are going away on our trip around the world for a saddening reason, I'm glad I'll be in your arms."

Lucas was having a hard time keeping his tears in, but soon he broke down.

Why did he have to let her go?

Eventually, he was able to gather himself, and he took a deep breath, not bothering to clean his face.

"Bethany . . . I love you so much." He sobbed a little but straightened himself up. "I will never stop loving you . . . and I'll never forget you . . . and I want to keep you forever . . . and I will. No matter what, we'll always be together. You'll always be in my heart and mind. And I . . . I'm so happy to be the one to be there if you begin to feel scared or alone. I'll be there. I'll be there to protect you. I'll keep you in my arms. I'll hold you and kiss you. I'll make sure there will never be a moment that you can feel scared. The next few days or weeks, I want to make sure you're absolutely comfortable and loved. I love you so much, Bethany."

Before anything else could be said, Lucas wrapped his arms around Bethany's body and held her close to him.

"I love you."

… … … … … …

Lucas and Bethany waved goodbye to their parents as they sat in the back of their limo. Lucas looked confused. "Where's this guy taking us? This isn't the way to the airport."

Bethany smiled sweetly at her new husband. "There's someone I want to introduce you to before we go. We have time."

Lucas nodded. "Oh okay. Who is it?"

"You'll see," Bethany said softly as she reached over to the side seat, patting Loki on the head.

The large Great Dane was lying lazily on the seat, groaning from tiredness. Lucas swore the dog was the laziest dog in the world. He couldn't believe they had to get a large limo just for the dog's comfort.

Bethany was showing Lucas around Manhattan a bit as they fought traffic.

Soon they pulled into a locked gated place. Lucas was confused. "Where are we?"

The security guard came up to the window, and Bethany talked to him but whispered in the man's ear.

Now Lucas was all the more confused.

The security guard nodded in understanding and went to talk to the driver, as if he were giving him directions.

At that moment, the gates opened, and the driver began maneuvering.

That's when Lucas realized where they were.

"The graveyard." Lucas sighed out, looking around at the thousands of gravestones placed everywhere in an organized fashion. "Oh no, no, no, no, no, I can't do this," Lucas begged Bethany, who took his hand. "Please, don't make me do this."

"You need to meet her," Bethany told him gently after the driver stopped in the children's area. "Come, come." Bethany opened the limo door herself and helped the fragile man out. "She's waiting to finally meet her daddy."

Lucas couldn't stop his tears from falling as he took Bethany's hand while she led him through one of the many rows of children's graves filled with flowers.

Bethany finally stopped under a gorgeous blooming cherry blossom tree, where a heart-shaped gravestone was hidden. It was covered in the shade with new sunflowers on her flowerpot.

Lucas sucked in a sharp breath as he read the cursive writing on the marble stoned heart.

Anastasia Rose Law

December 13, 2014

The Most Beautiful Little Angel Born on Earth

But Jesus Needed Her in Heaven More

Daddy's Little Girl

Mommy's Precious Baby

Grandma's Sweet Cupcake

Grandpa's Beautiful Princess

We Love You, Anastasia.

And then a precious picture on top of Anastasia's lifeless face, dressed up with a bow on her head.

All Lucas could do was fall to his knees in front of the grave and sob violently. "I just wanted to protect your mom. I failed her once. Now I'm failing her again!"

He felt Bethany's arms go around his torso and lean her head on his back.

"You failed no one, Lucas. You saved me. You're my hero." She leaned around his body, and he wrapped his arms around her waist, pulling her into his lap. She stared at Anastasia's picture with a smile. "I come here almost every day. I haven't come all week for obvious reasons. I still paid for flowers to be delivered biweekly, every Saturday and Wednesday."

Lucas nodded. "Okay, I'll keep that going."

Bethany looked back at him. "Really?"

"Yes," Lucas told her. "I am also glad to know where Anastasia is . . . so . . ."

"I was actually going to talk to you about that," Bethany said. "I already paid to be buried with her."

"Okay." Lucas kissed her cheek. "I love you. I don't want you to go."

Bethany couldn't answer as she hummed a sweet tune to him in a feeble effort to comfort him.

... ...

Lucas was sitting by himself in first class, no one around him, as he looked out his window. He had a cup of coffee to keep him awake so he could keep an eye on Bethany and Loki, who were in the row in front of him.

Loki lay down and had the seat almost reclining all the way back. Bethany was adorable as she was lying on top of Loki's chest, sleeping soundly.

Lucas was annoyed every time Loki would let out a huge yawn but tried to control his anger.

He focused on the storm going on outside. It was raining heavily. The plane seemed to be steady for now. It reminded him of the night in February of their senior year of high school.

Lucas was heartbroken.

Bethany was accepted to Julliard in New York.

It was always her dream to go there, so why wouldn't she?

He couldn't believe it. He was stuck going to UCLA because his parents wouldn't let him move away. Meanwhile, his girlfriend whom he loved with his whole being was going to be going to school across the country.

So he dumped her.

Yes, he was an idiot. He was so hurt and knew that it wouldn't last long distance, so he didn't want to wait for the broken heart.

So he broke it off.

He lied to her and told her he didn't love her after all. He didn't want to be tied down in college. And he said to enjoy New York because he wouldn't miss her.

It was devastating. He didn't stick around to see her cry.

Now he was in his room, crying himself, looking out the window as it was raining and storming, lightning and thunder, the whole nine yards of a depressing night.

It was odd. It was sunny and clear weather earlier that day, but the moment he broke up with Bethany, it started storming.

Spooky.

He knew he made a huge mistake.

He just didn't want his heart to be broken later, so he figured to give up then.

Knock, knock.

His bedroom door opened to reveal his mom. She came in. Lucas rolled his eyes and wiped away his tears off his face.

"Not now, Mom."

Suzanne smiled as she sat on his bed by the door. "Is that any way to speak to your mother? You may be eighteen now, but you're still under my roof."

Lucas groaned, "Not now, Mom."

"I noticed you deleted your social media page," Suzanne continued, regardless of his begging to be alone. "Care to explain? I love looking at pictures of you and Beth."

"Not anymore," Lucas grumbled. "I broke up with her."

Suzanne gasped, "Excuse me?"

"She was accepted to Julliard for her vocals and acting, Mother!" Lucas snapped, standing up and pacing around his room. "We would break up eventually anyways. I'm stuck here in California, while she'll go off and meet a great artsy guy in New York! Okay, so I figured to let her be free so she can date whoever she wants!"

"Lucas Simon Law, you know that's not true!" Suzanne told him. "That young lady loves you more than anything in the world! I know you love her too."

"I do, with all my heart, but I just don't want to deal with the heartache later." Lucas sighed. "I just want to get it over with."

"Son, you can't think this way. Love is a strong bond between two people that cannot be tarnished, unless you throw it away, like you are now," Suzanne said firmly. "I'm very disappointed in you for letting her walk away."

"Go away, please," Lucas groaned, leaning against the nearest wall.

Suzanne sighed. "Lucas, please listen to me! What will she do without you? You're her whole world."

Lucas rubbed his lips together and shrugged. "I don't know . . ."

"I think the better question is, what will you do without her?" Suzanne let him contemplate her question as she left the room, hoping that would knock some sense into him.

Lucas thought about her question.

What will he do without her?

Can he live without her?

He remembered the moment they met in tenth grade. Two years later, here they were. He didn't want those two years to go to waste.

If she were going to New York, then maybe things would be okay. They could video chat on the phone daily, text, and call. He could go visit her, and she could come home in the summertime and for holidays. With all that technology and airplane flyer miles, they could see each other daily!

He smiled, realizing they'll never really be apart!

But then he realized he just dumped her an hour ago.

He grabbed his hoodie and raced out his bedroom, passing his mom on the staircase in a hurry, and grabbed his car keys. He yanked on his combat boots and went to leave the house when he saw Bethany outside his door on his porch.

Her hair was soaked. She was dripping from her head to her boots. Her fist was up, as if she was about to knock. She gasped as the door opened, almost like it startled her.

They both stood in silence, but Lucas realized she was going to get sick.

"Mom!" he called up the stairs as he brought Bethany inside, watching her shiver. "Oh jeez, you're going to get so ill!" he scolded her as he grabbed a blanket from the hall closet and quickly put it over her after she took off her boots and jacket. "What were you thinking?" He wrapped her in his arms and held her close. His heart was racing with worry. "You could catch pneumonia!"

"I couldn't . . ." She shivered violently, unable to finish her sentence.

Finally, his mom was running down the stairs. "Bethany Marie Johnson, what are you doing?" she shrieked as she saw the young woman. "It's freezing outside! Oh my, come, come. Come upstairs. You can borrow some of my pajamas. Lucas, grab one of your hoodies with the fleece inside because that'll warm her up in no time!" She led Bethany up the stairs.

Lucas set out another blanket in the living room and turned on their automatic fireplace. He hoped it would be warm enough for Bethany when she returned.

When Bethany came back with his mom beside her, Lucas noticed her swollen red eyes as if they had been crying.

His heart shattered into a million pieces. He made her cry.

His mom smiled. "I think you both need to talk." She patted Bethany on the head and left them alone, closing the sliding doors to the living room behind her.

Bethany couldn't move from her spot, scared of Lucas.

Lucas admired her dressed in sweats and a long-sleeved shirt. Her hair was still dripping wet but not like it was before when she first came.

He motioned for her to come closer as he held up his hoodie. She timidly walked closer, and he put the sweater on for her, and she helped him a little.

After he knew she was warm, he stared into her scared brown eyes.

Bethany bit her lip before speaking. "Lucas, you didn't let me finish earlier at my house."

Lucas nodded. "You're right, I didn't."

"Even though I know we are broken up, and I know you meant what you said before about how you don't love me, nor will you miss me, I know you don't want to be tied down. I understand all of it. I won't hate you for it." Her voice broke as tears began coming down her cheeks. "I won't fight you on it, okay? I just wanted to finish what I was trying to tell you earlier."

Lucas stayed silent, no matter how much he wanted to plead for forgiveness and tell her that he didn't mean anything he said.

"I was accepted into Julliard, and my father is pressing for me to go, but I've already told my parents I'm going to UCLA with you, and nothing has changed, nor will anything

change," Bethany said, almost reciting her words. "My father is upset, my mother is proud of me, and I'm happy because I'll be with you."

Lucas's jaw dropped.

His stomach flopped.

Why did he have to be such a hothead and speak before thinking?

"Now that was going to be my speech from before, when you interrupted me after 'I was accepted to Julliard, and my father is pressing for me to go,' but I know we're over, and I'll respect your wishes." Bethany closed her eyes, unable to look at him. "I know you don't love me, and I understand. I won't bother you anymore. I just didn't want you to think I was leaving. I'm still staying. I'm going to UCLA."

Lucas gulped as Bethany tried to walk away, but he grabbed her hand and pulled her back to him, wrapping his arms around her. "Oh baby girl," he whimpered as she broke down and began sobbing into his chest. She couldn't hold her pain inside herself any longer. Lucas even let his own tears fall. "I didn't mean a word I said earlier."

Bethany gasped and leaned back, staring into his eyes, "Really?"

Lucas nodded, putting his hands on her face. "Yes. I meant nothing. I was impulsive. I didn't listen to what you said because . . . I was so proud of you, and I wanted you to go to New York, but I didn't want us to break apart while you were over there. I decided to break up now instead of later."

Bethany seemed to lose feeling in her legs to hold her up, so Lucas helped her onto the couch, wrapped her in the blanket, and sat next to her. She curled up to his chest as he held her close to him.

"Bethany, I love you. I would miss you. I am not tied down, never will be," Lucas told her inches from her face. "I didn't want to be in the way of your dreams."

"You are my dream," Bethany whispered to him.

"I know that now because you're my dream come true," Lucas *told her. "That's why I opened the front door to leave before you knocked earlier. I was leaving to go tell you that I made a huge mistake. And I was going to beg on my knees for your forgiveness." He grinned. "I can still do that if you want."*

Bethany giggled through her tears. "No, thank you, but I do forgive you."

"Bethany, I want you to go to Julliard though," Lucas said as he had a serious expression. "You worked your butt off your whole life to go to that school."

"I don't care," Bethany told him. "I can't be separated from you."

"Bethany . . ." Lucas couldn't let her give up her dream.

Bethany smiled. "No matter what, I'm going to UCLA."

Lucas didn't say anything for a while, instead pressed his lips against hers, kissing her passionately.

Lucas smiled at the memory as the storm seemed to clear up and the sun came out of the clouds.

The power of love, huh?

CHAPTER EIGHT

Hospice

June 11, 2017

When everyone from first class was led off the plane after landing in Santorini, Lucas honestly couldn't believe it was only 10:00 a.m.

It was night when they left New York. Now it's morning the next day. He felt like he missed a whole night of sleep.

He carried their carry-on bags, while Bethany held Loki with the leash and carried her purse. He thought it looked comical that a small girl like her was walking with a well-behaved dog that was almost to her chest, height-wise.

As they headed out of the airport, a man held up an erasable board that read "LAW" in a messy handwriting. The man was a short guy in a suit and looked to be excited to see the two as they walked up to him.

"Lucas Law! What an exciting day it is to be your personal driver, sir!" the man stated in broken English along with a thick accent. "I am a fan, so is my wife and three daughters!"

Lucas chuckled as Bethany was leaning down a bit to check on Loki, who looked to be scared of the business of the airport. He didn't realize everyone was trying to get a picture on their cell phones or cameras of Lucas. Thankfully, they were not rude and didn't bother them.

He didn't want Bethany to be trampled by fangirls.

"Thank you, sir," Lucas said kindly to the driver. "What's your name?"

"Isaias, Mr. Law." Isaias smiled brightly. "I am going to be at your disposal. Wherever you and Mrs. Law need to go, I will take you."

"Thank you, Isaias," Bethany said sweetly to him, keeping Loki close to her. "I hope you have room for our big monster here." She giggled, patting Loki's head.

"He's a big one!" Isaias said happily. "But I brought the long limo so the dog will be very comfortable." He suddenly took Bethany's carry-on bag out of her hand gently. "I'll take this for you, ma'am. No need for someone so beautiful to hold any bags!"

Bethany blushed. "You're too kind."

Lucas kept a protective eye out for Bethany as they walked through the crowds to get to the outside where the long limo was waiting in the pick-up area. Security guards were trying to keep fans out of Lucas's way as they made their way through to the limo.

As Isaias put all the bags in the trunk, Bethany let Loki get into the limo first for his safety.

Suddenly, a reporter came up with a recorder in her hands. "Lucas Law!" she yelled out, being held back by the security guards. Lucas turned to her for a moment as Bethany was about to get into the limo. "Is it true that your brand-new wife is dying?"

Lucas narrowed his eyes at the woman. "Does it make you feel better yelling that out to me like this?" he asked her in a harsh tone. Bethany put her hand on his arm, but he took no heed. "That is none of anyone's business of what's happening in my personal life right now! If you had any kind of soul within you, then I suggest you leave us alone and get your big story somewhere else!"

Bethany finally took his hand with both her hands and tugged him a little. "Come on, Lucas. Pay her no mind," she said softly.

Lucas wanted to continue his rant but realized that no matter what he said, no matter what the world reported, and no matter what anyone said or did, nothing was going to change. His new wife was dying, and she was days away from death, which is why they were in Greece, to make her comfortable.

No matter what this woman was going to say or do now, nothing she did would make anything worse.

He ignored the chaos around him as he helped Bethany gently get into the limo, and he slid in after her, slamming the door behind him.

Lucas was quiet on the way to the beach house he rented out for a few days or weeks. It's indefinite. Bethany was fussing over Isaias's reckless driving and if Loki was comfortable enough as they made the half-hour drive through Santorini.

He watched as Bethany cooed to Loki, who was just staring at her and enjoying her attention.

It was destroying him inwardly knowing that Bethany would be getting weaker and weaker as the week went on.

What made everything worse was the realization that he wasn't going home with her. Well, he was but not the same way they came.

Bethany told him that she wanted to die in Santorini, Greece, with Loki by her side and in his comforting arms.

It almost took him all his strength and willpower not to lash out.

Why wasn't she more devastated by this? Why was she accepting death so well? Why was she so content with leaving him alone?

As they arrived at the beach house, memories flooded his mind of their first visit.

Lucas walked out of the beach house to see the sun slowly setting over the waters. It was a beautiful sight.

What made it more beautiful for him was seeing his girlfriend of four years in a baggy sweater that was off the shoulder over her bikini suit. She was always so cold, even in the perfect weather here in Greece.

Lucas quietly walked out toward the water and sat down next to Bethany, who was sitting with her legs crossed, waiting for the sun to set.

She saw him and smiled. "Hi, my love. Enjoyed your nap?"

Lucas leaned over and kissed her gently on the lips. "Yeah, I did. When did you get up?"

"About half an hour ago," she answered as she turned her attention back to the scenery. "I felt like I needed some meditation."

One of the things he loved about Bethany was that she was a very holistic person and always believed in spiritual ways of healing, instead of taking a pill whenever you felt anything wrong.

He knew one of the situations bothering her at the moment were the small rashes forming in different parts of her body.

And that morning was tough because they suddenly found a few tiny red blotches on her face that resembled the rash on the rest of her body.

Bethany was always a person who cared about how she looked because she always wanted to be presentable. Seeing the rash forming on her face was almost traumatizing to her.

"Beth, we will see the doctor when we get home next week, but honestly, it's barely noticeable," Lucas told her, holding her hand and giving it a comforting squeeze.

"You don't get it." Bethany sighed, not wanting to face him. "It's not normal, and it's gross."

"Not gross," Lucas firmly said. "But you are right . . . It's not normal for you. I'm worried."

Bethany suddenly looked to him and smiled. "Worried? About what?"

Lucas shrugged. "I'm just worried that something could be wrong. I don't want anything to happen to you, babe."

"It's just a rash though," Bethany told him.

"You can't blame me for creating these weird illnesses in my head, Bethany," Lucas told her. "This isn't normal for you, and for it to just appear so randomly, it scares me. You're my whole world."

Bethany blushed. "I am?"

"Yes, of course," Lucas answered her. "I love you, Bethany. You've been in my life since I was sixteen years old. How could

I imagine life without you? I want to marry you someday, and I want to be with you forever. To ever imagine life without you is a nightmare."

Bethany leaned over and kissed his cheek sweetly, making him blush. "I love you too, but don't worry, I'm not going anywhere."

"You better not. I won't let you," Lucas told her as he wrapped his arms around her waist and leaned on her shoulder as the sun disappeared behind the ocean. "I can't live without you."

"But out of curiosity . . ." Bethany leaned on his head. "What would happen if you ever did lose me?"

His grip around her waist tightened, which didn't go unnoticed by Bethany, as Lucas gulped. "I don't know. I can, honest to God, say that I would have no idea how to live or even breathe without you. I pray that nothing ever happens. I pray God will always keep you safe and well."

Bethany kissed his hand. "I thought you didn't believe in God."

"God and I may not be close, but I do believe in Him," Lucas informed his girlfriend. "There has to be a God because He made the most perfect angel in the world who's sitting next to me . . . and even though He and I don't have a bond or relationship like you and God have, I still pray for your health and safety on a daily basis."

Bethany smiled. "Aw, my love."

Lucas softly kissed her forehead. "I love you."

Isaias helped Lucas get the bags into the entrance of the small beach house. Lucas paid and tipped Isaias, and Isaias said he would see them tomorrow.

Lucas saw Bethany sitting on the steps, facing the beach, looking very tired suddenly, as Loki was wandering the beach in front of the house.

Lucas put the bags into the bedroom before joining her outside.

By the time he returned, Loki was lying on the couch on the porch.

Lucas rolled his eyes as he sat down next to Bethany.

"He's the laziest dog in the world."

Bethany smiled tiredly at him. "What time is the hospice nurse going to be here?"

"In about thirty minutes." Lucas looked at his watch, seeing the time.

"Okay." Bethany sighed. "I'm so exhausted all of a sudden."

Lucas nodded, trying to hold back his emotions. "Let's go get you a nap. I'll handle the hospice nurse when he arrives, okay?"

Bethany shook her head. "No, I don't want you to have to deal with all that."

Lucas didn't take her answer as he stood up and helped her up carefully as she swayed a bit. He didn't want her to fall, so he picked her up gently into his arms, leading her into the bedroom. Loki watched them leave and slowly followed them.

Bethany was laid down on the bed, and Lucas helped her get under the covers of the large bed. Loki jumped on the edge of the bed and lay down next to her, giving her space as well. Lucas made sure his wife was comfortable before letting her lay her head on the soft pillows.

"It's not fair for you to have to deal with all the paperwork," she mumbled, attempting to keep her eyes open.

"Beth, you've already done everything," Lucas reminded her as he sat on the side of the bed, running his fingers through her hair. "You've already had everything set up before we arrived. You've made me your power of attorney years ago, so I'll make sure everything's fine. I'll make sure you're comfortable. I don't want you to be in any pain."

"I'm not," Bethany whispered, slipping to sleep. "I worry about you."

"Don't be." Lucas leaned down and kissed her forehead as she slipped off into a deep sleep. "I hope you're not in pain."

… … … … ….. …

As Lucas waited for the nurse to come, he was on the porch on the swing, reading one of Bethany's best books.

He couldn't believe he had never heard of Bethany's books until he had found her again.

The way she was so descriptive and detail-oriented in her writing blew him away.

He knew she was a poet, especially from high school and college, but this was taking everything to the next level, and she succeeded.

Soon there was a car that pulled up the gravel driveway, and Lucas knew it had to be the hospice nurse, and that's when his stomach dropped.

Seeing the male nurse get out of his car with a briefcase and a lunch pail that looked to have medications inside, it made Bethany's fate real.

The nurse saw Lucas on the porch and walked up the side steps to him.

"Hi, Mr. Law. I'm Ray Frantini. I'm the nurse who will be taking care of your wife for the next couple of days to weeks." He shook the hand of Lucas, who could barely speak. "I see you're keeping yourself busy with some reading."

Lucas nodded, shoving his hands into the pockets of his jeans. "It's my wife's book."

"Yes, I read in her file she's a well-known author in New York." Ray gave him a heartfelt smile. "May we talk inside?"

Lucas nodded once more, this time it felt numb. They walked inside and sat down at the tiny dining table that overlooked the ocean outside.

"Bethany is asleep," Lucas said as he motioned to the opened bedroom door. "She was drained of all her energy after that long plane ride."

"I bet she was." Ray grabbed some paperwork out of his briefcase. "So I wanted to discuss everything with you, and we can update Bethany later."

"I just have one question," said Lucas, not able to look Ray in the face. "Will you promise me that she won't be in any pain?"

"Patients of kidney failure typically don't have any pain," Ray explained to him. "Just in case, we will be giving Bethany some morphine every eight hours. I will come back at ten tonight and give her some, then tomorrow morning at six, and in the afternoon at two, although Bethany does have the right to decline it if she doesn't want it."

"Of course," Lucas agreed. "Will she get weaker?"

"Yes, severely." Ray nodded. "She will get more and more tired, less talkative, and very drowsy. She may not want to get up much, and between the kidney failure, recently getting off dialysis, and the morphine, she may stop eating. Meals may just make her nauseated. If she doesn't want to eat, don't force her to eat, or if possible, supply her with soup or liquids."

Lucas let out a shaky breath. He couldn't believe he was discussing his wife's death. "Oh."

Ray gave him a sympathetic look. "We will be prescribing Bethany with Lorazepam 0.25mg PRN, which will be given to her every eight hours. We just want to her to feel relaxed and calm, and we don't want her to feel anxious or scared."

Lucas nodded silently.

"One thing you should also know, Lucas, is that the morphine is strong," Ray warned him. "Morphine is the medicine that takes all the pain away, yes, but it shuts down your organs as it moves through your body. Every eight hours I give it to her, something will be shutting down. Her skin will get yellow, her pulse will get high, her blood pressure will get low, and she will feel very cold. She may get extremely sleepy, or she may just be asleep altogether when the time comes."

Lucas closed his eyes, gulping and holding back his emotions once more. "Oh god, I don't think I can do this."

Ray sighed, waited for him to be comfortable once more.

Lucas looked out the window. "I have been with that woman since I was sixteen years old. Yes, we have been separated for the past two and a half years, but I cannot live without her. I don't know. I, honest to God, cannot tell you how I lived without that woman for the past couple of years. Now that I have her back, though, I don't know how I am supposed to simply fly back to New York to plan her funeral and live my life like she wasn't there!"

Ray nodded. "This won't be easy, Mr. Law."

"When we were twenty years old, she asked me what I would ever do if I ever lost her," Lucas rambled on, seeming to be in his own world. "I told her that the only—*the only*—time I have ever talked to God was to pray for her safety and her health. The only time! I told her I had no idea what I would do but that I prayed to God every day that she would always be alive . . . and that her heart would beat for me. How do I go on without her?"

"Lucas . . . sometimes God does things we cannot comprehend, why He is doing the things He does," Ray told him. "Perhaps this world is too small for Bethany. God may need her help in Heaven."

Lucas stayed silent for a minute, thinking over Ray's words. "So God gave the world an angel, Bethany, and He may need her back home."

"That's how I look at it," Ray answered. "Perhaps since this world is so sinful and dangerous, perhaps God just wants her home where she'll be safe from the violence."

Lucas smiled at Ray. "Thank you."

"Lucas?" They heard Bethany's weak voice from the bedroom.

Lucas got up immediately and headed over to Bethany's side within the room, leaving Ray there. "You're awake. I hope we didn't wake you up," Lucas said hastily as he helped Bethany sit up.

Bethany sighed and shook her head. "No, I had a nightmare. I was scared."

"Nightmare?" Lucas frowned.

"You were hurt, and you needed help. I couldn't get there in time." Bethany looked upset. "I felt like I failed you."

"Oh, sweetheart." Lucas gave her a small smile and fixed her hair a little for her. "I'm here. I'm fine. I'm not leaving your side."

"Promise?" Bethany smiled sweetly at him.

Lucas leaned over and kissed her temple gently. "Promise."

Suddenly, they heard a knock on the open bedroom door, and they both saw Ray standing there, looking awkward. "I'm sorry to disturb."

"No, no, it's fine." Lucas motioned for him to come in, and Ray came to them, holding out his hand for Bethany to shake. "Babe, this is Ray Frantini. He's the hospice nurse."

"Nice to meet you, Mr. Frantini," Bethany greeted as she shook the man's hand. Ray then took a seat in the lone chair across them. "Hope the house wasn't too difficult to find."

"No, no, Mrs. Law, it was quite easy. It's beautiful," Ray told her as he took out his laptop. "May I ask a few questions?"

"Of course." Bethany nodded, holding Lucas's hand tightly with both of hers.

"I know you've already done all the paperwork, but I still want to get to know you, Mrs. Law, your past, and of course, your relationship with your husband," Ray told her, typing on his laptop. "Now it says you are in stage 4 of kidney failure and the end stages of lupus."

"Unfortunately, yes." Bethany sighed. "I've tried everything to fight, but nothing worked."

"I see," Ray said as he was typing everything down. "When were you diagnosed with lupus?"

"I was nineteen years old, the summer before my sophomore year of college at UCLA," Bethany said solemnly. "I didn't take it seriously back then."

"Not many people do, considering it starts out as a rash," Ray assured her. "So how long have you two been a couple?"

"Technically, almost ten years," Lucas answered. "We met the day I turned sixteen and received my driver's license."

"Now, is there any history of depression or any type of mental health issues in the family history?" Ray continued.

"Yes, my mom had depression. My grandmother did. Most of the women in the family had severe depression," Bethany told him. Lucas nodded, already knowing about that. "I've also had depression." He knew that too since she was diagnosed with depression in the eleventh grade.

"Any past attempts of suicide?" Ray asked, looking up at Bethany as he waited for her answer.

Lucas answered for her. "No."

"Actually . . ." At this, he sharply looked at his wife, who hid her face from him, staring at their hands. "Yes."

"What?" Lucas gasped out. "You've been lying to me?"

"Lucas, between telling you about my lupus, me going missing, telling you about the death of our daughter, and the reality that I'm dying from kidney failure, I just figured that was enough for you to deal with!" Bethany snapped. "I just wanted to protect you!"

"Well, you're not!" Lucas told her. "You're hiding things from me!"

"Lucas, I lost my daughter!" Bethany began whimpering, making Lucas try to attempt to stop his rampage. "You didn't know about it, and I was so alone over there, and not to mention, you were doing so well in modeling, so I just left you alone! But I felt so heartbroken, so I swallowed a bunch of pills."

Lucas went pale. "Oh dear god!"

Bethany continued, not able to look anyone in the eyes, "I convulsed. My landlord found me dying on the floor of my bathroom. I was in a coma for a few weeks. After I woke up, I was put in a mental institution."

Lucas was shocked. "I can't believe this."

"That's where I figured out my love of writing. I wrote a whole book in that mental institution. While I was in there, the nurses brought in someone who wanted to publish my book. They wanted to help me start over. That's exactly what I did."

Ray was amazed at her strength to bounce back so fast after such a traumatic event. "Wow."

"And then I found Loki, moved into my loft. I wrote book after book, and some days I would go without eating because I was writing so much. I drowned myself in writing. I didn't want to face the fact I lost my daughter and you didn't know about it, so I disappeared from the world, from everyone. I changed my name. I became a new person." Bethany sighed. "I'm sorry, Lucas."

"Don't be." Lucas finally was able to get the words out. "I should've been there for you."

Ray leaned back in his chair, looking very intrigued. "It looks like you both still have quite a bit of honesty to do."

"I guess so," Lucas said, feeling very exhausted suddenly.

He was starting to wonder how much more his heart could take.

"Let's continue." Ray tried to break the tension. "Are you okay to continue, Bethany?"

Bethany wiped away her tears. "Yes."

"Okay, now you said you lost your daughter," Ray hinted.

"I was mugged and beaten almost to death when I was eight months pregnant. My daughter, Anastasia, was stillborn,"

Bethany confessed to him. "I was heartbroken, not only for losing her, but also I felt like it was my punishment for not telling Lucas."

Lucas felt like his heart shattered at her words. "Beth, no, no, no . . . baby, no, you weren't punished, I promise. You did nothing wrong. I understand why you didn't tell me."

"Bethany, where were you beaten the most that night?" Ray asked.

"Well, my stomach, of course, and my back. He continuously stomped on my back." Bethany flinched at the memories.

Lucas narrowed his eyes at Ray. "Why?"

"Well, you know, this could've been why the lupus came on so strong in the past couple of years," Ray explained. "Between giving birth to a stillborn and then having your kidneys kicked over and over. Now that your lupus came back with a vengeance, it went fast because your kidneys have been damaged so from the beating."

Bethany nodded. "Wow. Yes, you're right. That's what the nephrologist told me."

Lucas closed his eyes, feeling lightheaded. "I just wish I was there."

Bethany couldn't say anything to comfort him, and she knew that, so she just rubbed his back gently.

… … … … … …

It took a while, but Ray eventually finished his questioning and began to explain to Bethany his schedule.

He set her up and began to get the morphine ready to give her.

Lucas sat on the bed with her but fussed over her, trying to keep her comfy.

Bethany giggled as Lucas kept fluffing her pillow. "It's soft, baby. It's soft." She sat up with his help as he put the pillow behind her. "I'm sure the least of our worries is the way the pillow is fluffed."

"It's a big one for me," Lucas teased her. "I want you to be a comfortable as you possibly can be."

"I am, I promise." Bethany smiled at him. "You and Loki are all I need." She motioned to the big dog, taking up half the bed.

"Eh, that's great," Lucas grumbled, making the large dog give him a grunt. "Feeling's mutual."

"All right, Ms. Bethany." Ray came back in with a small pill. "This is your morphine pill."

Bethany stared at it for a while, realizing this was the pill that would shut down her inner organs slowly. It would also ensure that she would not have any pain.

She took a deep breath and grabbed the water bottle next to her bedside. She took a drink of the water and then grabbed the pill.

She stared at it for a minute before putting it in her mouth, swallowing it with the water. She felt it go down her throat.

"Now that you've taken the first pill, we have to keep on schedule, or you could end up getting some drastic withdrawal." Ray was writing something down on his tablet. "Withdrawals are worse than anything."

"Okay." Bethany nodded.

"I'll be back here at nine tonight," Ray told her. "My job is also to make sure you're comfortable, even though I'm sure Lucas has that covered."

"I'll take care of her," Lucas whispered. They could tell he was distraught from her taking the first dose of morphine.

"Okay." Ray put his tablet to his side. "I'll be going now. Please make sure you try to keep something on your stomach. Maybe soup or something soft."

Bethany sighed. "I'll try."

"There you go." Ray nodded and went to leave.

Soon Lucas jumped off the bed and went after him. He walked Ray out to the porch.

"Give me the truth," Lucas demanded in a soft voice, not wanting Bethany to hear anything. "How long do you think?"

"Lucas . . ."

"I'm asking is because I cannot be taken by surprise," Lucas told him. "I just need a . . . I don't know, something!"

"Take a deep breath," Ray told him, and Lucas did so. "I'd give her maybe about a couple of days. She's pretty weak. It's hard to say though."

Lucas nodded, feeling his heart break. "Okay."

"Stay strong." Ray put a firm hand on his shoulder. "I'll see you in eight hours."

"Yeah," Lucas said as Ray walked back to his car. Lucas watched him leave their beach house, and he swore he felt his soul dying inside.

A few days?

That's it?

Lucas let a tear fall from his eyes. He wanted more time than that.

"Lucas."

Lucas's head snapped up, and he quickly wiped away his tear as he saw Bethany in the doorway. She was dressed in a baggy T-shirt and short shorts, with her hair messily in a ponytail.

She looked to be glowing in the sun's rays.

Lucas couldn't help himself as he walked up to her and pressed her small weak body against the door frame.

He couldn't stop himself having his way with her in that moment.

He didn't care anymore.

He needed one more time with her. He just wanted to feel one with her once more.

He threw her on the couch and made passionate, rough love to her, and she responded back with sweet kisses.

He just needed to be in her once more, to feel her once more.

CHAPTER NINE

Waterfall

June 12, 2017

Sometime during the next morning, Bethany was up before Lucas, him being tired from their spontaneous lovemaking the night before.

She tucked him in and motioned for the awake Loki to follow her out the bedroom door. After feeding him, she went to the bathroom. She pulled down her underwear, realizing she didn't need to pee very much. She was dehydrated. As soon as she was done and she brushed her teeth, washed her hands, fixed her hair a little, she left the bathroom.

She let the glass doors open toward the beach, and Loki ran out to relieve himself.

She stepped out and let the cool summer air of Greece hit her, and she took a deep breath of the ocean air, letting it settle in her lungs.

If she didn't already know she was dying, she wouldn't suspect it. It was a beautiful feeling being in front of a clear blue ocean, with white sand everywhere, surrounding their small beach house.

Just being there made her feel as if she were healed.

Bethany walked up to the steps that led to the sand and stepped down with grace as she pulled up her long nightgown so she wouldn't get it too dirty. She let the sand go between her toes, and it felt soothing to hear, walking in the coolness.

She watched as Loki was running around, chasing some seagulls in the distance. He wasn't bothering anyone, except the seagulls.

She walked closer and closer to the clear waters, and finally her feet were touching the ocean. It felt almost amazing.

She heard stories before about people who were in their last days wanting to take a trip to the ocean just to feel the breeze or touch the water.

She understood now why they wanted that.

It was a magnificent feeling.

Once more, she breathed in the ocean air and heard Loki barking. She looked over at him and saw him running after the seagulls that were trying to get away from him.

Bethany giggled as she walked slowly after him. She had never seen Loki so free and happy. Soon she realized that Loki was too far off, and she huffed, "Loki! Wait for me!" She used all her strength to run after the hyper dog.

Soon she caught up to him as he was lying down almost half a mile from the beach house. "Loki!" She giggled as she collapsed next to him, out of breath. She laid her head on his stomach as he panted to cool down. "Great, Loki, now I'm too tired to walk back."

The dog groaned as if he didn't really care.

She laughed at his reaction and sat up with his help. She looked around and saw a small hut. It read TOURS.

"Hm." She was curious as she stood to her feet and walked toward the hut. Loki decided to follow her, not leaving her alone. She still felt very tired, so she leaned on the large dog a bit.

… … … … … …

Ray decided to let himself in after seeing the door opened, figuring they were awake.

"Hello? It's Ray! Hospice nurse!" he called out toward the kitchen.

He set his briefcase and the lunch pail that contained the medicine on the dining room table and walked toward the kitchen, seeing no one there. He saw that the dog food had been slobbered on not too long ago.

"They have to be awake," he mumbled as he walked toward the bedroom door. He sighed, closing his eyes.

"Please don't be having sex, please don't be having sex," he prayed to himself as he finally peeked in, but he just saw Lucas in bed. "Oh, thank God."

He walked in, knocking on the door. "Lucas, sir," he greeted loudly.

No response.

He raised an eyebrow as he knocked louder. "Mr. Law!" he said sharply, hoping that would get him up. Still nothing.

"Americans can sleep through anything, I swear," Ray muttered as he walked closer to Lucas, seeing him drooling on the pillow under his head, taking over most of the bed.

"Mr. Law!" he said, close to Lucas's ear, but Lucas suddenly let out a large snore, startling Ray.

"Dear Lord, man, wake up already!" he snapped as walked out of the small bedroom.

He decided to just look for Bethany, who was nowhere in sight.

"Beth?" he called out, looking at the bathroom, but it was dark.

He checked the whole house, no sign of Bethany or Loki. He walked out to the porch again, but nowhere on the beach did he see Bethany.

"Oh great." He smacked his forehead with his hand and went back to the bedroom, where Lucas was still snoring away.

"Wake up!" he shouted into Lucas's ear.

Still no response, so he grabbed the glass of water on the nightstand close to the bed and, without a second thought, threw the water onto Lucas's face.

Lucas jumped away and startled awake. "Whoa, what the hell? What's your problem?" he yelled to Ray as he was trying to regain himself.

"Where's Bethany?" Ray asked, unfazed by his anger.

Lucas froze and stared at Ray. "Why are you asking, 'Where's Bethany?' when she's supposed to be here?"

"Well, she's not," Ray simply stated as he left the bedroom. "She needs her medicine, Lucas!" he called out as he went toward the kitchen.

Lucas was worried and grabbed a shirt to put on over his pajama pants, running outside. He searched around the house, not finding anyone.

"Loki! Come here, boy!" He whistled and called out for the dog, hoping that if he came, then he would find Bethany.

He went toward the water and finally found footprints and pawprints heading toward the shop he found the last time he came to the island.

He sighed in relief as he jogged over there.

Once he arrived at the shop, he went inside, and the moment he closed the door behind him, Loki walked up to him. "Hey, boy," Lucas greeted the large animal and walked past him.

He found Bethany reading some brochures with a middle-aged man showing her some pictures. "Babe." Bethany looked startled and turned around, gasping at the sight of Lucas. He didn't care, but he wrapped his arms around her petite body. "I'm so glad you're okay."

"I'm sorry, sweetheart, I didn't mean to worry you," Bethany told him, looking up at his concerned face. "I was hoping to be back before six, but I guess I took a detour."

"I was just showing this young lady around Santorini and some places you newlyweds should check out," the man said, smiling at Lucas.

Lucas sighed. "Sadly, we can't. It's not that kind of honeymoon."

Bethany looked at him. "What do you mean?"

"Beth, you're not strong enough to go sightseeing," Lucas told her. "You're currently missing your medicine right now."

"Please." Bethany held his hand. "I want to do something big."

"Like what?" Lucas asked in disbelief. "Aren't you Miss Play-It-Safe?"

"I'm dying, Lucas," Bethany stated. "I don't fear anything anymore."

Lucas sighed deeply. "Babe . . ."

"Nothing can hurt me the way lupus has," Bethany continued. "It's taken over my life since I was nineteen years old. Help me fight back. Sure, we won't win the war, but maybe we can win today's battle. Let's do something to beat today."

Lucas looked her in the eyes and saw her pleading look. "You have a point. I want to help you win one battle and every battle after, but I just don't want you in pain."

"I'm not. I promise. I'll let you know when I am." Bethany gave him a pouting look.

"Oh jeez, who would say no to that face than a heartless monster?" Lucas chuckled as he kissed her lips. Once they released, he sighed. "All right, let's see what's up, and then we have to go take your medicine."

"Then we can go?" Bethany asked.

"Then we can go, for sure," Lucas told her, kissing her forehead. "Even Loki can go."

Bethany laughed. "I don't think he'll want to." She pointed at the large dog in the middle of the place, lying down, sleeping. "I let him wear himself out earlier. He'll be out for the rest of the week!"

Lucas rolled his eyes. "Lazy dog."

"Your wife was looking at this hiking guide." The man tore Lucas's attention away from Loki. He handed Lucas a map. "It leads to a waterfall where people like to go to face their fears."

Red flags everywhere. His wife was too weak for this hike. His wife was not strong enough for jumping off waterfalls. And worst of all, his wife was dying!

Unfortunately, he knew he wasn't winning this one.

"Let's go after breakfast." Lucas forced a smile as Bethany seemed excited.

After walking back to the house, Bethany rushed into the house and saw Ray, who was enjoying a cup of coffee and reading a book from their bookcase.

Bethany smiled. "Hi, Ray, I'm here! Sorry for making you wait!"

"Anything you for, Mrs. Law." Ray smiled at her, putting the book and cup of coffee away. "Where's your snoring husband?"

"I HEARD THAT!" a shout came from the porch.

Bethany couldn't hold in her laughter as Lucas came stumbling in, carrying the 120-pound dog in his arms as if he were carrying a child. The dog looked completely content. Soon Lucas made it next to Bethany, falling to his knees and dropping the dog on the carpeted floor. The dog lazily went to the couch to lie down, while Lucas was panting and sweating on the ground.

Bethany smiled while patting his back. "There, there. Are you okay?"

"I'm fine," Lucas grunted.

"What can I do to help?" Bethany teased him as Ray shook his head in amusement.

"Nothing," Lucas said, not being able to hold his head up.

"Do you want a treat for being a good boy?" Bethany giggled.

Lucas finally couldn't control himself as he burst into a fit of laughter along with his wife. She wrapped her arms around his neck, and he took one of his arms, pulled her by her waist on his lap, and hugged her tight.

Ray smirked at them. "You guys are insane but made for each other."

And that's what made this situation much sadder.

... ...

Isaias picked the couple up around eight, so they could get a head start on their journey. They had only until two because that was when Ray would be back at the house for her next dose of morphine. As they pulled up to the entrance of the hiking route, Bethany seemed quite excited.

Lucas a bit more nervous, but he wasn't going to stand in the way of her chance to have an adventure one last time.

Isaias helped Lucas get their backpack out of the trunk and smiled. "I will be back here around one thirty."

"Sounds good, Isaias," Lucas said as he helped Bethany out of the car after putting the backpack on his back.

As the car left them there, Lucas knew there was no going back. He took her hand as they began the path up.

They walked for a few minutes in a comfortable silence, letting Bethany take a good look at everything.

Lucas watched her walk a bit ahead of him so she can see things closer and smiled at her.

She was wearing black skinny jeans with black and white tennis shoes, which made her look adorable. She had on a gray hood that fit her figure quite well, while her hair was up in a messy bun, her face a bit sunk in, which was expected to happen after they stopped dialysis.

In his eyes, she was the model in the relationship, not him.

Soon she came back to walk next to him and grabbed his arm, leaning her head on it. He loved when she did this.

When they first became a couple, guys who always hit on her didn't want to believe or didn't respect them enough to back off. To protect herself, Bethany would wrap her arms around his arm, indicating he was protecting her.

Those memories always made him feel like he still had some purpose in this world because before he found his career in modeling, Lucas always felt like he was her bodyguard.

Word spread like wildfire that next week. Their second date after the dance, Lucas jumped the gun and asked Bethany to be his girlfriend. To his surprise, she said yes.

They made it "social media official," which meant everyone knew.

When Lucas entered the school, hand in hand with his new girlfriend, who didn't seem to notice all the eyes on them, his stomach sunk.

He didn't like attention too much.

He walked Bethany to her locker and kissed her cheek, letting her go to her class so he can go to his.

He went to his first class of the day, which was his biology class. He sat next to his table partner, who stared at him.

Lucas raised an eyebrow at his partner. "Need something, Nate?"

Nate shook his head, adjusting his thick glasses. "No, just curious."

"About?"

"How did you get a date with the Winter Princess Bethany Johnson, the most popular girl in school?" Nate asked in disbelief. "It's really strange. Did you guys ever talk?"

"No," Lucas answered, a bit annoyed. "We met at the dance on Friday."

"She talked to you?" Nate was confused. "I don't understand, she's popular! You're a geek like me."

"Thanks for that." Lucas sighed. "Anyways, she's a really awesome person. Maybe, if everyone in this school would take the time to get to know her, you all would see her how I see her."

"Sounds gay to me." Nate shrugged. "So what are you going to do about Thomas?"

Lucas narrowed his eyes at Nate. "Thomas James? The quarterback?"

"Yeah, he was the Winter Prince." Nate looked worried. "He is very verbal how much he likes Bethany."

"So?" Lucas shrugged. "I don't care. He wasn't fast enough. Besides, I really feel something special for Bethany."

"Eh, I'll give you guys a week," Nate stated as the teacher came in.

After a few classes, it was time for lunch, and Lucas decided to head over to Bethany's locker to see if she wanted to sneak off campus for lunch. In their school, only juniors and seniors could go off campus, but no one really cared.

He grabbed his car keys from his locker and then saw Bethany at her locker, talking to Thomas. She looked uncomfortable as the guy looked to be pleading with her.

"I don't understand why you've been putting me off for so long, and then you are suddenly together with that new guy," Thomas said in an annoying, whining voice.

Bethany leaned against her locker, looking to have a headache. "Thomas, please, I don't want to keep repeating myself. I've been telling you for months. I don't see you that way."

"How is it that this new kid comes along so suddenly and you're in love with him?" Thomas pressed on.

"I don't know." Bethany shrugged. "The second I saw him, I felt he wasn't like anyone else. I talked to him and found out he was different. He wasn't a follower. Like me."

"I'm not a follower, Bethany," Thomas told her, stepping closer to her. "I'm a leader."

"Back up, please," Bethany groaned. "You're wearing too much cologne, and it's choking me."

"I don't understand why I never was able to get a chance," Thomas persisted.

Bethany smiled. "Because I'm not looking for dating or flings. I'm looking for a relationship. The moment I met Lucas, everything felt right."

"But—"

Lucas had had enough. He walked toward the two as Bethany was still trying to get Thomas to step away from her. He broke the two and stepped between them, facing Thomas. He was the same height as him, but Thomas was much stronger.

"You must be the new kid," Thomas grunted at Lucas.

Lucas didn't look fazed. "Yeah. Lucas Law."

Thomas chuckled. "Lucas Law? What are you, a model, a stuntman?"

"Look, man, leave Bethany alone." Lucas ignored the insults, which really didn't sound like insults to him. "She's with me now. She's being polite and trying to turn you down nicely."

"You don't deserve a hot chick like her," Thomas told him. "She's the hottest girl in school, so she needs to be with me. That's why we were voted Winter Prince and Princess. Everyone wants us together."

Lucas was disheartened. Maybe they should be together.

But when he felt Bethany's small arm wrap around his arm as a sign of protection to her, he knew it helped her feel safer. He wanted that. He wanted to be her protector, her bodyguard.

That's when Lucas stood tall to Thomas who backed away a little at Lucas's newfound courage.

"I'm with Bethany because we aren't into stereotypes or how we look. Yes, she is gorgeous, I don't know why she said yes to be my girlfriend. I'm the weird, new kid with a ponytail, ugly glasses, and I dress weird, but you know what, she did. And I'm happy. Being with her means having a best friend forever. She's more than a girlfriend. I can already tell we're soulmates." Lucas sighed. "So go find someone else. Bethany said her piece already."

Bethany smiled brightly at Lucas, giving his arm a light squeeze of support.

Thomas rolled his eyes. "Whatever. She's not worth anything anyways."

Before Bethany could react to those words, Lucas had Thomas pinned to the locker.

"Lucas!"

"Don't say she's not worth anything because this girl is worth everything," Lucas growled into Thomas's face.

He let him go, and Thomas grabbed his stuff, taking off to his next class.

Bethany sighed. "Lucas, are you trying to get kicked out?"

"He won't bother you anymore, Bethany." Lucas ignored her question. "I won't let someone disrespect you."

Bethany smiled at him. "Thank you for defending me and saving me from that annoying back-and-forth conversation."

Lucas gave her a firm nod.

"Hey, when you said all those mean things about yourself, I disagree," Bethany told him, taking his hand into hers once again.

"What do you mean?" Lucas asked out of curiosity.

"You're not the weird kid. You're perfect," Bethany told him. "Your ponytail is totally awesome. Your glasses make you sexy, not ugly. Your style for clothes is unique and urban. I love everything about you. Like I told Thomas earlier, I like you because you're not a follower."

Lucas blushed. He felt his heart melt at her words.

That's the moment he knew he loved her.

"Babe?"

Lucas snapped out of his memories at the sound of Bethany's voice calling out his name, and he looked to her. "I'm sorry, my love. I zoned out there."

"I could tell." She giggled. "What's on your mind?"

"Just thinking about all those times when you would hold my arm like you are now," Lucas told her, motioning to her tight grip. "You always did that back in high school, when Thomas never stopped harassing you."

"Oh my goodness, I forgot all about Thomas!" Bethany exclaimed. "I remember him. Oh my, that was so long ago."

"He thought that since he was the quarterback, he could have whatever he wanted," Lucas stated. "He couldn't have you though."

"Nope." Bethany smiled. "I was taken . . . Remember the time he was so upset one day he broke into my car to wait for me, but we were actually already in the back seat making out!"

Lucas laughed. "Yes, I do remember that! His face was priceless."

Bethany realized they were soon close to the waterfall when she saw the shimmering waters beyond some trees. She gasped and pointed, "Look, babe!"

Lucas stopped in his tracks, along with Bethany, and took in the view of the beautiful miniature lake that had a waterfall. The large rocks that led to the waterfall were put in such a way it looked to be almost landscaped. The sun peeked through above trees that hid the small piece of paradise, making everything seem to glow.

"Isn't it the most beautiful thing you've ever seen in your life?" Bethany asked, still in awe.

Lucas shook out of his gaze and chuckled. "No, it's not. I know one person in my life who takes that trophy."

Bethany saw that he stared at her with a smile, and she rolled her eyes. "You're still such a charmer after all these years."

The couple went closer down there and saw no one else was there, and they were silently thankful for that.

Soon they were into their bathing suits, and before Lucas could say a thing, Bethany ran to the waterfall, climbing up a long line of rocks that led to a ledge.

Lucas wanted to call her back; he wanted to stop her.

Why was it he wanted to protect her from getting hurt when she's jumping off a ledge into a lake when he can't protect her from lupus?

Lucas waited there and even took out his phone to take a recording of this moment.

He wanted to share the moment his wife faced her fear of dangerous stunts just because she wanted to protect her incurable disease of lupus; she was going to jump off that ledge into the lake below her.

Nothing was stopping her.

As he zoomed in on her catching herself before almost falling backward, his heart stopped, but then he relaxed as she waved at him from her spot on the very top ledge.

She was close to the top of the waterfall.

She even went to the edge and felt the water, smiling as she did.

Lucas couldn't help but adore the sight.

A ray of sunshine was hitting her body, and she seemed to sparkle in her light pink bikini.

It took her quite a few minutes, and as she stared down at the shimmering body of lake water beneath her, she seemed to have second thoughts.

Her fears were coming back.

Finally, she looked to Lucas and shook her head, letting a tear of failure release from her brown eyes.

Lucas shook his head before she started to come down by climbing the rocks.

"Go, Bethany!" he shouted up at her, and she stopped in her tracks, looking at him. He smiled at her, trying to give her encouragement. "You have nothing to fear anymore, right?"

Bethany smiled back at him after thinking over his question and then nodded.

She stepped back a few steps, and suddenly, before his eyes and his recording video, Bethany ran to the edge and jumped off.

No second thoughts, no fears, nothing to hold her back.

Lucas held his breath once she hit the water with a splash and waited for her to come up, zooming in on the spot she went into the water.

He waited a good twenty seconds before she finally came up to the surface to catch her breath.

She waved to him and the camera, smiling brightly.

He was so proud of her.

He pressed "end recording" on his phone and turned it off, putting it in his bag before running into the water, joining Bethany. He swam in and took her in his arms, and she wrapped her arms and legs around him.

They said nothing as they stared into each other's eyes.

She ran her fingers through his wet hair with one hand and the other she was massaging the back of his neck.

Lucas enjoyed the feeling of her hands massaging his head and neck, making him feel so relaxed than he had felt in years.

"Hey, babe." Bethany attainted his attention with her soft voice. He opened his eyes as she stopped massaging his muscles. "What's your plan?"

"How do you mean?" Lucas asked, keeping a gentle grip on her body close to his.

"What's your plan after I pass?" she whispered to him, attempting to be careful around this delicate subject.

"I've sort of thought about it, but I've always stopped myself." Lucas sighed deeply, leaning forward a bit and putting his chin on her shoulder, letting his lips wander her neck gently. "I feel like I'm signing your death certificate if I think about stuff like that."

"You're not, my love." Bethany kissed his cheek, running her fingernails along his back with care. "It's something you have to think about. You have to go on after me."

"I don't want to though." Lucas felt his emotions beginning to lose control as his eyes began to burn from holding back his tears. "Why does this have to happen? I went through two and a half years without you in my life, why must I lose you once again? But this time, I can't get you back."

"You'll always have me in your heart, Lucas," Bethany told him. "I'm sure you'll take Loki and go back home."

"To New York," Lucas told her. "I want to stay in New York."

"You sure?" Bethany leaned back a little, but he kept his grip on her hips to keep her up. "Your career is in California."

"I don't want that anymore though," Lucas told her. "I want to be alone in New York in your loft so I can feel you everywhere. I want to have Loki there and take him for walks in that park close to your place. I want to . . . I want to be a motivational speaker."

Bethany's eyes widened once he said those words. "What?"

"Yes," Lucas admitted. "I want to travel and tell people your story."

Bethany gave him a small smile. "My story?"

"I want to tell the world how amazing, gracious, and strong you were," Lucas explained his new life goal to her. "I want to always be talking about you. I want everyone to hear of you. I want your name and your spirit to be spread to the world and everyone's hearts."

Bethany looked to have tears gathering in her eyes as she put her hands on his face, caressing him lovingly. "Oh, Lucas . . ."

"I want to take some English classes and learn to write. I want to continue your legacy," Lucas confessed. "I read all your books while just being here for a full day. You're an amazing writer, and no one could compare to you . . . I will never be able to write like you, but I want to write about you. I want to write your life story. I want to write our love story. I want to write how you battled lupus for years. I just want everyone to know how much of a miracle you were."

Bethany smiled and pecked his lips, letting their foreheads stay connected for a while. "I love you so much. You are, by far, the strongest man alive."

"No, I'm not," Lucas mumbled. "I'm still dying inside. I want you to stay with me. Giving you up, I know God needs you more in heaven, but I want you to stay here with me."

"Lucas . . ."

"I know it's selfish, but I literally just found you. Why can't you stay?" Lucas's voice broke. "I feel like life is punishing me, or at least it's tormenting me."

"You can't think that way," Bethany told him.

"But that's how I'm always thinking," Lucas confessed. "I feel like life has been picking on me and nothing can go my way."

"You're a famous model," Bethany pointed out the obvious. "How can you not be grateful for that?"

"Bethany, I don't care about that stuff." Lucas seemed to be getting upset. "Haven't you been listening?"

"I have, but I think it's extremely selfish of you not to be happy about having the career everyone dreams of having," Bethany told him sharply as she left his arms and swam to shore.

Lucas growled and went after her, swimming to the shore and stomping up to her as she grabbed one of the towels to dry off. "Really? So you ask me a question and we end up fighting? Is that really what's happening?"

Bethany sighed. "Lucas, I just don't think you should talk bad about your life! Your life is so amazing! You have a great career! You're wealthy, probably have an amazing place in Hollywood, and now you'll have a pretty nice loft to live while you're in New York!"

"Because of my career, that tore me away from you!" Lucas suddenly snapped.

Bethany froze and looked to him in bewilderment. "What? What are you talking about?"

"If I didn't stay behind in California for my career while you moved to New York, and if I didn't stay two thousand miles away from you for all those months, maybe we would've been better off today!" Lucas shouted at her, almost viciously, trying to get his point across. "If I had been less selfish, put you first, maybe we would be a family with our daughter!"

Bethany was heartbroken at his words.

No matter what she could say to him, nothing will change his mind.

He'll always blame himself.

Lucas was worried that he had frightened her or upset her. "Beth?"

Bethany held back her tears as she put her clothes back on.

"I want to go home."

Lucas gulped. "Back to New York?"

"To Heaven," Bethany muttered, facing away from him.

As she continued to get dressed, Lucas felt defeated. Here it was, probably their last-ever outing together, and he ruins it. They'll never get that time back.

CHAPTER TEN

Masterpiece

June 15, 2017

Tension filled the beach house after the couple's argument that seemed to break Bethany's heart.

Bad part was Lucas didn't even know what he did wrong.

What was so bad about him blaming his career on missing out on having a family with Bethany?

He wasn't wrong.

If he hadn't put himself first all those years ago, he and Bethany would have their daughter, and Bethany would be healthy.

They were twenty-two, and they were about to get married. How could anything be wrong with it? They would've been a beautiful family.

Why couldn't his wife just accept his feelings on this?

It had been three days since their argument, and things haven't been good at all.

Bethany gave up.

She quit eating, she didn't want to go outside for fresh air, and she was in bed the entire time.

She didn't want to talk with her husband or Ray.

The only living being she wasn't pushing away was Loki, who was attempting to comfort her as much as he could.

Bethany's weight decreased severely. She was so much thinner in her face, and her body seemed to be almost skin and bones.

She didn't want to look Lucas in the eyes, knowing that she was literally killing herself. She was giving in to lupus, kidney failure, and the morphine that was slowly shutting down her organs.

She knew it.

Instead of having a week with her, Lucas was afraid he would only have today left with her.

She now had oxygen on her to keep her breathing, but that's only for comfort. Her heart will stop when it has nothing left to keep it pumping.

The terrifying part of the whole ordeal was Lucas wondering if he was going to watch his wife pass away today while she was still upset at him. Could he let this happen?

After being separated for so long, could he really let her die without giving her love and support?

As Ray came out of the bedroom, Lucas stood up from his spot on the couch and begged silently for good news, but Ray just shook his head.

Lucas frowned, letting his head hang. "It's soon, isn't it?"

"She is not verbal anymore," Ray told him, standing before him, trying to keep his own emotions in check. "But I don't think that's the medication or the kidney failure. Why did you have to upset her so?"

"All I did was tell her the truth," Lucas told him. "She wanted to know how I felt, and I told her."

"Maybe that truth that you think is correct is wrong," Ray suggested. "Maybe you are filling your heart with lies."

"I left her in New York, all alone, and then she was attacked and gave birth alone to our stillborn daughter," Lucas sneered to Ray. "How is that not my fault?"

"Did she know she was pregnant when she moved to New York?" Ray asked.

"Well, no."

"Did you know?"

"No."

Ray rolled his eyes. "Lucas, are you psychic? Of course, you are not psychic. You need to get over this and move on. You are refusing to let your grief go. Therefore, you are letting Bethany suffer."

"I don't want her to suffer, but I know if I had been there for her, everything would've been fine," Lucas reasoned with Ray.

Ray stared with disappointment at Lucas and then sighed, gathering his things. "I'm sad to hear that. I was hoping you would let go of the past for your dying wife to help her heal mentally and emotionally while letting her lean on you physically as she dies, but I guess not. I guess your made-up guilt is enough for you to feel," Ray sneered. He gathered his briefcase and lunch pail. "I'll be back at six. The chaplain should be here in a few minutes."

Lucas took in his words and then realized what Ray said. "Six?"

"Yes. I will come at six, and then I'll be staying here." Ray looked remorseful. "She won't make it through the night."

As Ray walked out of the beach house, Lucas gulped and felt his heart break.

She won't make it through the night.

The time Lucas had been dreading was here. He stared at the closed bedroom door and wanting nothing more but to go in and hold her close to him, just wanting to hear her heartbeat.

He had been dreading this moment. Now it was here.

… … … … … …

Lucas sat on the couch, looking directly into the bedroom that was open, as the chaplain was sitting in the chair next to Bethany's bedside, reading her the Bible and praying with her once in a while.

Bethany's drained eyes were closed, but her hand was petting Loki's head softly as he was lying on her lap. Her eyes were sunk in a bit and darkened around them. Her hands were looking a bit on the yellow side, showing signs of her organs failing.

Soon the chaplain, who was dressed in a regular suit and had his black hair to the side, took Bethany's free hand into his.

"Now, Bethany, please tell me how you are feeling."

Bethany opened her eyes a little and looked to the man. "Scared."

"Scared of death?" the chaplain asked her.

She nodded timidly.

"My dear, there's nothing to fear when you'll be going into the hands of God."

"I'm just scared of leaving my husband," Bethany admitted in a quiet voice. "What if he doesn't move on from this?"

"Your husband just wants you to not be in pain," the chaplain told her. "He knows where you'll be going, and he knows you'll be taken care of."

"He blames himself for everything though," Bethany told him.

"Ah well, some men take on that impossible responsibility and guilt. They feel they've done something terribly wrong when their wife is hurt or in trouble," the chaplain explained. "He wants to protect you, but he cannot this time."

Bethany nodded. "I just hope he finds peace."

"As long as you make sure you find the peace, he'll eventually find his," the chaplain told her and patted her knee to comfort her. "Pray for him."

Lucas had to leave and walk around on the patio, unable to fathom the amount of emotion he was feeling.

His wife was dying. She was dying, and the only thing she was thinking about was him.

How selfish could he have been?

"Lucas."

Lucas turned to the doorway, seeing the chaplain standing there with his Bible in his hands and straightening out his suit.

"Father."

The chaplain motioned for the outdoor couch for Lucas to sit with him. They both sat down and sat in silence for a bit.

Lucas gulped, scared of the conversation.

"Father, the hospice nurse estimates that my wife won't make it through the night."

"That is God's timing, not his," the chaplain said strongly, staring at the ocean waves hitting the sandy shore before them. "Look at that wave, Lucas."

Lucas looked confused as he stared where the chaplain was staring. "The wave?"

"All of them. Every single one of them." The chaplain motioned to the scenery before them. "They are just beating that beautiful sandy beach, correct? Those waves show no mercy."

"I don't understand," Lucas said, not wanting to hear about the nature around them. "My wife is dying. What does this have to do with my heart breaking?"

The chaplain went silent once more before continuing, "This beach house is sturdy. It's the best I've seen in all my travels. Everything is so protected, but what exactly is going to protect this beach house from those waves?"

Lucas stared at the chaplain in disbelief. "What?"

"The sand is. All those tiny pebbles of sand, those billions of little grains of sand surrounding this house, are absorbing the waves. They don't let those waves come any closer until the waves get too overwhelming. Sometimes, Lucas, the waves will jump over the sand to get to the house, and it will wipe out the house."

Suddenly, Lucas seemed to be putting the pieces together in his mind. "The sand can do everything it can, but the waves will take down the beach house, even when the sand did everything it could possibly do. The pebbles of sand did everything they could, but they can't control the outcome."

Chaplain nodded. "All the sand can do is be there for the aftermath, bring comfort to the beach house. It's damaged, and it's torn to pieces. Sometimes the house has just been destroyed, no life in it, but even after the storm, let the house know the sand will never leave it alone. The sand will wait for the house to appear once more . . . even if it's in another place."

Lucas felt his tears involuntarily fall from his eyes as his heart felt so full once more. "What if the sand just wants to go with the house?"

Chaplain sighed. "It's God's timing, God's plan. God's will be done."

"I just wish I understood why she has to go," Lucas's voice cracked as he began crying, facing away from the chaplain. "I understand now . . . I get it . . . but . . ."

"Lucas, you are the sand." The chaplain put a hand on Lucas's shoulder. "You have taken everything that's ever come at you two in your relationship. Bethany has told me that you protected her through the small things and the big problems."

"I've tried so hard," Lucas croaked.

"She said that even though everything around her seems to be fading away, the only thing she stays strong by is the fact you kept up your strength," The chaplain told him. "No matter how you feel, no matter how you think you failed, just know that the house knows how much the sand took the beatings and hardships just to keep the house safe. Bethany loves you so much for taking the stress off her during the last ten years of her life."

Lucas tried to wipe his tears away with the back of his hands, but only more slipped out. Soon he gave up trying to clean his face. "But, Father, I didn't even do that much this past few weeks!"

"Were you not the one who came from California to New York to find her?" the chaplain asked. "Were you not the one who took her to dialysis?"

Lucas shrugged, not wanting to act strong. "It was only a few times."

"Lucas, were you not the one who set up hospice? Planned the wedding ceremony? Set up plane tickets? Taken care of Bethany night and day since you've arrived here?" the chaplain kept pressing the subject. "Bethany even said she's had a hard time controlling her bladder, but you don't get upset or disgusted. Instead, you just get her into a warm bath and clean up after her. You dress her and brush her hair for her, and you don't say a word about it."

Lucas closed his eyes, remembering every moment the past couple of days. Has their relationship been really strained? Or was it just in his head? Has he really been so blinded?

Has he actually been helping more than he thought he was?

Yes, last night. Bethany woke up crying and in agonizing pain.

She had wet the bed. She was screaming from embarrassment and demanded him to leave the room because she was so humiliated.

It tore him to pieces to see her that way.

He remembered going to the bathroom and getting the bath going for her. He made sure it was perfect temperature. He remembered going back to the bedroom, seeing her on the floor.

She fell, and she was too weak to get back up.

She was curled up, holding herself, sobbing violently.

He couldn't hold his tears back as he remembered undressing her out of her wet nightgown, and she screamed at him to not touch her because she was disgusting, but he refused to ignore her.

He remembered picking her up into his arms, feeling her almost weightless body.

He remembered feeling her spine, being very visible on her back.

Her rib cage was showing.

Her shoulder blades were sticking out.

She looked so weak.

She was still crying as he slowly put her in the tub.

He remembered her big sigh of relaxation after she rested her back into the tub. He then went to the bedroom and put all the sheets in the washer. He grabbed some new ones from the closet and put them on the mattress. He remade the bed, so it'll be nice and warm for her. He grabbed a new nightgown for her as he walked to the bathroom.

She was struggling to wash herself. He pulled up the sleeves of his long-sleeved shirt and helped her.

She was still crying as he gently put the soap on her back and rubbed it with his hand. He massaged her back at the same time.

Soon she was cleaned up, and he assisted her out of the tub.

After putting a new nightgown on her, he helped her into the bedroom and laid her into the bed, wrapping the blankets around her fragile body.

She didn't even open her eyes after laying her head on the pillow.

She fell asleep so fast.

He remembered falling on his knees, praying for his wife to not feel any pain.

The chaplain knew that Lucas was remembering the night before and smiled.

"You have made her last days on earth very comforting. She is not scared of dying, Lucas. She's scared of scaring you."

"I don't want her to be worried, Father."

"Then give her comfort," the chaplain told him. "Not just physical comfort . . . Try emotional. Let her know that you'll be okay."

Lucas looked to the chaplain and nodded. "I will."

"Good man." The chaplain sighed and stood up from the couch. "I'll be taking my leave now."

"Good day, Father," Lucas said as he left.

Lucas leaned back and kept watching the waves.

He closed his eyes, feeling the warm breeze come against his skin.

He didn't want this moment of peace to go away.

As Lucas shut his apartment door behind him, he smiled to himself as he received a letter from the jewelry store that he ordered their wedding bands from.

They've arrived.

The last thing they needed for their wedding were the bands.

In a few weeks, he would be moving to New York.

In a few weeks, Bethany would officially be Bethany Law.

He was so excited to be married to the love of his life. He couldn't ever imagine anyone else he would rather spend his life with than Bethany. She was just so gorgeous and kind, along with being so supportive.

She was his princess.

She was such a masterpiece.

He looked at his watch. It was four o'clock here.

It's 7:00 p.m. in New York.

He figured it wasn't too late to call over there. She wouldn't be on her way to her friend's place yet to celebrate Thanksgiving over dinner.

Yes, it was Thanksgiving. He was so depressed not to be spending this holiday with his future wife, but he knew that they would be together for Christmas.

He pressed on Bethany's name on his cellphone and let it ring a couple of times before he heard her voice answer.

He couldn't stop his smile.

"Hello, handsome!" Her happy voice came from over the phone.

His heart melted. "Hi, my love," he smoothly greeted her, trying to not sound sad for not being able to be with her on their favorite holiday. "How's your day?"

"Hmmm, kind of lonely." She sighed. "But I'll be leaving to my friend's house in about half an hour."

"Babe, please, please, please be careful going there," Lucas told her. "You told me last night you haven't been there yet, and it's in a sketchy part of New York City."

"I'll be all right, Lucas, don't worry," Bethany told him. "I'm not going anywhere without you."

"So I have a surprise!" Lucas exclaimed. "The mail came, well, the mail came sometime this week, since I haven't checked it in like three days."

Bethany could be heard giggling over the receiver.

"Anyways, the wedding rings are at the jeweler," Lucas told her. "I'll pick them up tomorrow, first thing in the morning."

"Ooh, yay!" Bethany said excitedly. "Now we are all set for our wedding!"

"Yes, girl, we are!" Lucas shared her enthusiasm. "Your dress, my tux, the decorations, the pastor, blah, blah, blah, we have everything now!"

Bethany was laughing by now. "You are so silly, Lucas."

"Only for you." Lucas calmed himself and smiled once more. "I miss you so much."

"Only a couple more weeks, babe," Bethany told him. "I'll be back in California with you, and then we'll be here."

"Yeah, I already have a few people saying they can get me modeling gigs over there," Lucas told her as he fiddled with the letter. "We'll be all set."

"You'll love our new apartment, but I'm not telling you where it is yet! It's a surprise," Bethany teased him.

"Ah, babe, I hate surprises!" Lucas chuckled.

"It's going to be great," Bethany told him. "I cancelled my checking account because you said that you wanted a joint account."

"Yes, that's right," Lucas told her. "Ah, man, everything is in place! I'm so excited!"

"Me too, baby. Me too." Bethany sighed. "I better get going to my friend's house."

"Please text me when you get there so I know you're safe," Lucas pleaded with her. "I just need to know you're safe . . . I don't want to ever not know where you are. I just want to know you're safe at all times."

"Oh, Lucas, how I wish you were here now." Bethany sounded to be tearing up. "I miss being in your protective arms."

"When you fly back here in two weeks, I'll never let you out of my sight," Lucas told her, trying to be strong for her.

"You're going to the day of the wedding though," Bethany reminded him. "It's bad luck to see the bride."

"Yeah, yeah, yeah." Lucas chuckled. "Besides that."

Soon their laughter died down once more.

"I love you, Lucas. More than anything in the world," Bethany told him. "I can't wait to spend the rest of my life with you. Nothing could take this away from us."

"I agree." Lucas held the phone close to his face, wanting to go through the phone just to be in her presence. He sighed deeply. "I love you so much, princess. You're my masterpiece."

"I'll text you when I get there," Bethany said. "Tell your parents I said hi, and Happy Thanksgiving!"

Lucas opened his eyes after the memory faded away.

That text never came.

The next morning he picked up the rings, and he called to tell her, then texted. He called. He called again. He texted and texted and called and texted.

It was almost three years before he heard her voice again.

Lucas realized he needed to be inside with Bethany.

With a heavy heart, Lucas stood up and went into the house. He saw the clock was already almost six o'clock.

Ray would be back soon.

Lucas walked into the bedroom and saw Bethany looking at Loki, who was asleep on her chest. She had her hands limply on his head.

Her chest was having trouble rising up and going down.

Lucas wanted to run, run far, far away. He just wanted to keep running. If he hit the other end of the island, he wanted to swim. He wanted to keep swimming, running, and even fly away.

He didn't want to be here.

He was scared to say goodbye.

Lucas gulped as he sat in the chair the chaplain was sitting in before, and he managed to get her attention.

Their eyes remained locked for the longest time until Lucas managed to speak.

"I understand now."

Bethany smiled at him. "You do?" Her voice croaked out.

Lucas saw that her oxygen tubes were a bit crooked, so he adjusted them back so they were directly in her nostrils.

He took her weak, cold hand. He saw it was a pale yellow color.

"I wanted someone to blame for this, for everything. I blamed myself for not being there for you. I blamed . . . you . . . for not taking lupus seriously all those years ago. I wanted to blame the guy who attacked you."

Bethany's eyebrows raised.

"Yes, even him. I blamed him for inducing this." Lucas felt his tears coming down once more. "I blamed your dad for not fighting for you like I did. I blamed the media for spreading rumors. I blamed the doctors and scientists for not having a cure or surgery or a medicine to save your life." He sniffled away some tears, but only more came. "I blamed us for not getting married sooner. I blamed us for not staying together all those years ago. I blamed us for agreeing for you to move away so early. I hate both of us for not being able to fight this."

"You hate us?" Bethany asked.

"Yes, because I wanted us both to fight this," Lucas told her, unable to recognize his own voice. "I wanted us to both come out of this, and you'd be healthy, we'd marry and live forever together. And then I would die the day before you did because I would not want to go on one day with you."

Bethany took her hand and put it to his cheek. "Lucas."

He felt her hand touch his cheek, and he couldn't stop himself from leaning into her touch. "I just wanted us to be together forever."

"We will," Bethany whispered. "In spirit, I'll always and forever be in your heart."

Lucas looked at her in the eyes. "Forever and always?"

"Yes." Bethany then took a deep breath, trying to relax, but it wasn't working. "I'm scared."

"Of?" Lucas asked, a bit worried.

"Of death," Bethany told him. "What if it hurts to die?"

"God won't let you be in pain, Beth." Lucas hated this subject, but it was the inevitable. "God's going to take such good care of his favorite angel."

Bethany sighed. "I wish I could stay with you."

"Beth." Lucas rubbed his lips together, trying to hold his emotions in.

"Now I have to go up to heaven and watch over you and watch you go on with your life. Meet someone. Have kids. Live this perfect life without me." Bethany suddenly made herself whimper.

Lucas shook his head. "How dare you say such a thing? I'll never move on from you."

Bethany sighed out her tears and rubbed his hand. "Lucas, you're a young man. You deserve to move on with someone else."

"Stop it, please." Lucas buried his head in her arm. "Please, stop saying those things to me. I'm getting physically ill of thinking about ever being with another woman."

Bethany took her free hand and ran her fingers through his wild hair.

Lucas sobbed into the sheets, gripping her arm, probably bruising it. She paid no heed.

"I have been with you since I was sixteen years old, and you were the first girl I kissed, made love to, hell, even the first girl I held hands with!" Lucas told her in a heartbroken tone. "I don't ever want to be with anyone else but you . . ."

"Just promise me that after I die, you'll put yourself first," Bethany suddenly said to him. "I want to die not worrying about you. I want to be in peace. I want to know you'll always be happy."

Lucas looked up at her and took her hand off his head and kissed her palm. "I promise. For you, Bethany Johnson—I'm sorry, for you, Bethany Lou, I will forever remain happy."

"Thank you." Bethany sighed.

Soon Ray came in and saw the scene. He smiled and patted Lucas on the shoulder. "I'm proud of you."

Lucas looked up at him and nodded. "I finally realized what you and Bethany meant."

"Good."

Ray checked on Bethany's vitals, so Lucas stepped aside, waiting by the door.

"Are you in any pain?"

Bethany just stared at him, breathing in and out heavily. "No."

Ray stared at her, sitting on the side of the bed. He felt her pulse, counting.

"Blood pressure is 70/40. Pulse is 138 beats per minute. Respirations are 12. Temperature is 104.8. Oxygen level is 78, even with the oxygen tubes," he mumbled as he typed it in his laptop.

Soon he gave her the injection of morphine since he knew Bethany wasn't going to be able to swallow the pill.

Lucas began shaking.

"Ray."

Ray looked at him with remorse. "Sit with her, Lucas, tell her what she means to you. Tell her you love her, let her know you are here. Don't stop talking to her."

Lucas closed his eyes, knowing what that meant.

This was it.

As the sun was setting, Ray opened the windows a bit. Apparently, it would help when she passes, so her spirit wouldn't get trapped in the house. Ray also offered to take Loki outside.

Lucas figured he only offered because it was hard for him to watch someone pass away.

He didn't blame him.

Instead of sitting in the chair, Lucas took Loki's place next to her and curled up to her.

He wrapped his arm around her, guarding her.

He ran his fingers gently through her hair and wrapped his other arm around her waist, pulling her closer to him.

She was conscious.

Her jaw was limp, though, while her eyes were wide open.

He felt she was staring into his soul.

But really, she was just staring at him.

Her hands and legs her limp, so he adjusted them so she would be comfortable.

Soon she was comfortably against his body.

He wrapped the blanket around them both, so she wouldn't feel cold.

"I'm here, my princess," Lucas whispered to her, knowing she could hear him.

He let his tears fall freely. He gently rocked her back and forth.

"There's one last thing you should know. The day we met at the dance, I was planning on killing myself after the dance. I wanted to die. My parents had moved me to a new town and put me in a new school, where everyone hated me. I was bullied, teased, and tormented because of the way I looked."

He saw her blinking at him.

She was listening.

"But then I met the most beautiful, remarkable angel that night," Lucas told her, cradling her tightly in his hold. "You gave me the will to live. So instead of hanging myself, I took you out to a diner. We stayed out so late. We cruised around in my dad's convertible. You made me feel like this is how it should be forever."

Lucas felt one of his tears fall onto her cheek, so he gently wiped it away.

"Bethany, this is how I know our love story does have a perfect ending. Boy meets girl. Girl saves boy's life over and over and over again, and even though girl is dying, boy will forever be saved by the girl because she'll be with him in spirit," he whispered to her. "I love you so much. I want to say thank you for saving my life. Thank you for showing what it is to be loved. I don't want to let you go, but, Bethany, I know you're hurting. I know you're ready."

Lucas sobbed as he rubbed his face to her cheek, sobbing lightly.

"I'm letting you go . . . You can let go, my love. Don't be in pain. I'll see you once again in heaven, I promise . . . You can let go . . . I love you so much."

Not even a few minutes after he said those words, Bethany Lou passed away on June 15, 2017, at 6:15 p.m.

CHAPTER ELEVEN

Everlasting

Unknown . . .

Pictures of Bethany appeared on the screen in front of the audience that was waiting patiently for their speaker tonight.

Pictures of Bethany and Loki together.

Pictures of Bethany at her book signing.

Pictures of Bethany with her parents.

And finally, the album of pictures of Bethany and her husband Lucas from ages fifteen and sixteen to a few days before she passed away.

Soft harp playing was going through the speakers as Lucas waited for his cue to go on stage.

Everyone who helped him set this up was compassionate and patient with him. This has been a vulnerable time for him, but Lucas surprised everyone.

He was so ready for this.

He told Bethany exactly what he was going to do: become a motivational speaker and tell the world about Bethany Lou, the famous author.

He wanted everyone, including her fans, to know the real her; how sweet and kind she was yet how raw and emotional she was.

Soon the slideshow was over, and a single photo of Bethany's professional picture was up. She was smiling so brightly at the camera.

Oh, what Lucas would give to have that face in his life again.

"Please welcome, Lucas Law, model, aspiring author, and motivational speaker," a voice came from the stage.

Lucas walked on stage as an applause came from the audience. Lucas shook the man's hand, and the other man went off the stage as Lucas set his notes up at the podium.

He sighed into the microphone and looked out into the audience.

"Hello, my name is Lucas Law. I am the widower of Bethany Lou, the famous New York author who spread her words of encouragement to those all over the world," he said professionally. "I married my wife June 10, 2017. My wife died of complications from lupus that caused her kidneys to fail on June 15th, 2017."

The audience were so wrapped up in Lucas's story, Lucas swore he could hear a pen drop.

Lucas cleared his throat before continuing, "My wife was born in Temple City, California. It's a small town close to LA and Hollywood. She was the most beautiful girl in school, yet she kept to herself. She didn't want friends because she had been bullied. She just didn't want to deal with the pain. She was fifteen years old. I had been living in Sacramento, California, before my parents dragged me to Temple City. I was an outcast. No one liked me. No one even cared that I was alive, that is, until it was my sixteenth birthday, and I just received my driver's license."

Lucas sighed. "I was suicidal because I thought that my high school career would be spent lonely now that I was moved to a new school and all alone. I didn't want to live because no one accepted me. I was a nerd: thin ponytail haircut, scrawny figure, ugly face, and severe acne." He shrugged. "I didn't even believe I was special, but she came over to me and handed me a cup of punch." Lucas smiled. "She saved my life that night."

Lucas continued on after taking a drink of his water. "We dated from the ages fifteen, sixteen, and were together until she passed away at the age of twenty-five. We were inseparable before we graduated from college. She moved to New York City after college graduation and after we became engaged." Lucas chuckled. "You would think that meant to take a hike, right?"

Everyone laughed.

"But we had everything planned out before she left. Everything was going smoothly for our wedding in the winter. I would move to New York after we said 'I do,' and then we could live happily ever after," Lucas scoffed. "I was so naïve. I thought nothing could stand in our way . . . While I was in LaLa-Land, Bethany had found out she was pregnant with our first child after she moved to New York."

Everyone gasped.

"Yes, I know, I didn't know about it at all." Lucas frowned. "She knew me so well, trust me. She knew the second she would've told me about the baby and her pregnancy, I would've let go of my career and gone across the country to be with her. So she kept it a secret. She was going to surprise me at Christmas." He sighed. "Except on Thanksgiving Day 2014. Bethany was attacked, beaten so severely. She was forced to give premature birth to our stillborn daughter, Anastasia."

Everyone seemed to be speechless, and some were crying in the audience.

"Afterward, Bethany was still terrified to tell me what happened because she thought I would hate her, so she disappeared. For two and a half years, she disappeared and left me behind. No one would search for her, thinking she ran away. Let me remind you I didn't know about the death of our daughter," Lucas told them. "I went in search of her. I even hired a private investigator. Soon the case went cold, but my PI refused to give up on Bethany. Neither did I. I couldn't fathom giving up on the woman I loved so much."

Lucas rubbed his lips together. "When I found her after so long, everything seemed to be able to go back to how it was, happy and in love, but then the next day after I arrived, Bethany was diagnosed with kidney failure stage 4 due to complications of her lupus disease. She had been battling lupus since the age of nineteen. I let go of my career just to care for her. She didn't like it, but I was so happy to just be near her."

Lucas closed his eyes, feeling the pain in his heart.

"I wanted nothing more than to have given up my kidney for Bethany, but unfortunately, the doctor stated she wouldn't even survive the surgery, let alone a transplant."

Almost everyone was crying now.

"I don't regret anything in our life though," Lucas explained. "I think by the time Bethany passed away, I was free of any darkness or fears. She wasn't in pain or scared. She is free in heaven. She is now safe with God. She's protected by the light around her. And I can live knowing she's safe. I think not knowing where my fiancée was just agonizing and completely nauseating to live with for two and a half years. Knowing where my wife is now, I just can't help but give thanks. She's pain free, and she's safe and sound."

Lucas continued to tell them, "The point I am trying to get across here is that people have to take a chance on one another. Let me tell you a story that my dad told me: 'Boy and girl meet in high school. Boy and girl go to college together. Boy and girl separate to pursue careers. Girl goes missing. Boy never stops searching for her and never gives up hope. Their love goes stronger as they are across the country from each other. Boy finally finds the girl and saves her.' And I really like that version, but let me tell you what the truth is . . ."

Lucas cleared his throat once more before continuing, "Boy meets girl. Girl saves boy's life over and over and over again, and even though girl is dying, boy will forever be saved by the girl because she'll be with him in spirit."

Some people in the audience nodded in agreement.

"I learned that no matter how much I tried to be her hero, or how much I felt sorry for myself, that Bethany was the center of it all. She was the strongest, bravest person I had ever met in my entire life," Lucas told them. "We can all learn from Bethany Lou. She was courageous, no matter the chances she took to hide her bravery. She was amazing."

Lucas smiled. "A wise man told me once the waves will traumatize the sandy beaches, but when the beaches do everything in their power to stop it, they still go over the beach and takes the beach house on it . . .

"You see, I am the sand, battling and protecting Bethany, the house, from the terrors the waves could bring on. Unfortunately, I may not always be able to save it, and someone's house will be destroyed all the way, but at least that means I know I did everything in my power to save her."

Everyone was getting chills at Lucas's words.

"Now think about this: I was not at all a believer in God before all this . . . well, sort of. I prayed to Him about Bethany because He had graced her so well in her life. Now that Bethany has passed on, I believe because I've seen all the timing that has occurred in this, no one on this earth can convince me now that there isn't a God.

"God is so real because He led me to Bethany right before she found out that she would die. How uncanny is that? God really knew what He was doing. Sure, I would love it if my wife were still with me, I really would, but God knew she was going to be much better off with Him in heaven.

"So what I'm telling you guys is that don't question anything in your lives," Lucas told everyone in the audience, who were listening closely. "You can't do it because if you do, you'll be missing on the time God has given you."

Suddenly, everyone began clapping at his speech, almost getting to their feet.

Lucas gave them a nod. "Thank you, thank you so much. I know Bethany thanks you all as well."

After saying his conclusion, Lucas walked off the stage and checked in with his new manager before leaving the building out the back door.

He jumped into his car where Loki was relaxing in the front passenger seat.

Lucas chuckled, watching Loki yawn. "How's my boy?" He rubbed the dog on the head. He started the car's engine and began to drive off out of the back parking lot and out onto the street. "I say we take off, Loki."

"Bark!"

"Let's get out of here." Lucas sighed, driving onto the nearest freeway. "Let's go wherever Mommy leads us."